KILL 'EM ALL

A TRUE STORY OF ABUSE, REVENGE AND THE MAKING OF A MONSTER

RYAN GREEN

For Helen, Harvey, Frankie and Dougie

Disclaimer

This book is about real people committing real crimes. The story has been constructed by facts but some of the scenes, dialogue and characters have been fictionalised.

Polite Note to the Reader

This book is written in British English except where fidelity to other languages or accents are appropriate. Some words and phrases may differ from US English.

Copyright © Ryan Green 2019

All rights reserved

ISBN: 9781079438048

YOUR FREE BOOK IS WAITING

From bestselling author Ryan Green

There is a man who is officially classed as "**Britain's most dangerous prisoner**"

The man's name is Robert Maudsley, and his crimes earned him the nickname "**Hannibal the Cannibal**"

This free book is an exploration of his story...

★★★★★ *"Ryan brings the horrifying details to life. I can't wait to read more by this author!"*

Get a free copy of **Robert Maudsley: Hannibal the Cannibal** when you sign up to join my Reader's Group.

www.ryangreenbooks.com/free-book

CONTENTS

Lost at Sea 7
Born to the Mud 13
The Painting Room 19
Off the Rails 27
The Trail of Ashes 38
Idle Hands Make for the Devil's Work 48
More Weight 57
Best Served Cold 68
A Normal Man 77
Heart of Darkness 87
The Boys of Summer 96
The River Pirate 106
Dannemora 116
The Big Time 127
Hurry It Up 133
Want More? 138
Every Review Helps 139
About Ryan Green 140
More Books by Ryan Green 141
Free True Crime Audiobook 145

Lost at Sea

Carl wanted him before he even knew why. There were plenty of sailors in the bars of New York each night, and there was a lot to be said about the appeal of a man in uniform. Even just the appeal of the uniform itself had been enough to tempt Carl into some bad decisions over the years, but none of that mattered compared to the confident smirk and the cocky stroll that he spotted across the room. This little bastard thought he was the king of the world. He thought that his pressed uniform and cleft chin gave him the run of the place, that he was going to live forever and feature as the highlight in the daydreams of every man, woman and child he crossed paths with. Carl had met plenty of men like that over the years, and given enough time, he had broken every single one of them.

There was no sweeter sound in all of the world than the little animal moan they made when all their illusions about the world fell away. When they realised that the thin veneer of civilisation could be stripped back so easily to reveal the savage truth beneath it. Carl loved to educate them. All these young, strutting, upstanding citizens who thought that the world owed them something more than pain. He loved to be there when they realised there was a power in this world greater than their own. That power wanted them to suffer.

Of course, he was too well-practiced to make his interest in this new boy known. If he came on too strong, they'd get threatened and scurry back to their barracks with their tails between their legs. Carl had to tease them along, wait until they were well into their drinks and work out just what kind of pressure he needed to apply to get them to come away with him. If they'd grown up poor like him, it was a simple matter of flashing some cash and making them an offer for their help on his boat. The poor boys were the easiest to spot, always paying too much attention to keeping their shoes so they could dance properly.

Once you moved beyond those that could be had for a flash of green, there were sodomites aplenty in the navy who could be persuaded to join him for no price at all beyond the promise of his predatory grin. He liked them the best because they had the most to lose if even a whisper of what he planned on doing to them got out. Of course, he would have had no shame tarring all the other men that he raped on his boat with the same brush, but these ones couldn't even pretend it was a lie. They'd rather deny that they had gone with him at all than admit that they liked it up the ass. He could turn them loose after he was done with them, if he so desired. Not that he ever desired that.

The last lot were harder to pin down, but were all the more satisfying to Carl when he got them; the cocky boys like the one who had just strolled in. You had to ply them with liquor, bolster their ego, wheedle them a little. It was all one great, grand balancing act to convince them that it was somehow in their best interests to come do a day's sailing. A day on a privately owned yacht during their leave, to earn enough walking around money to make the rest of their shore leave enjoyable. Carl talked it up like it was a party more often than not, that they'd barely be doing any of the sailing at all, that there would be loose women and booze flowing freely. There would be booze on his ship, but

Burke's first official military press credentials were signed by Walter Bedell ("Beetle") Smith, General Dwight D. Eisenhower's Chief of Staff at Allied Forces Headquarters, North Africa on April 25, 1943.

O'Connell covered both the North African and Sicilian campaigns before arriving in Florence, and frequently found himself assigned to photograph the Supreme Allied Commander as part of his official duties.

(O'Connell collection)

The main stage of the former Army Pictorial Center located in the heart of Long Island City, Queens, New York.

(National Archives)

Col. Melvin E. Gillette, the "architect of Military Pictorial Service" organized and directed Fort Monmouth's first training Film Field Unit in 1937 and the first Training Film Production Laboratory in 1940. When the laboratory was moved to Long Island City in 1942 and was incorporated into the new Signal Corps Photographic Center (SCPC), Long Island City, New York, Col. Gillette became the Center's first commanding officer. Gillette served as the Army pictorial representative on Gen. Dwight D. Eisenhower's Allied Headquarters staff in North Africa and as photographic officer with the Fifth Army in Italy under Gen. Mark Clark. Col. Gillette returned to San Francisco in January 1947, suffered a heart attack that July and died on Sept. 11, 1947. In 1948, the Pictorial Center of the Presidio, San Francisco was dedicated in his memory and named the Gillette Pictorial Center. Colonel Gillette is buried at Arlington National Cemetery, Washington, D.C.

Signal Corps Photo #41-TFL-16E, National Archives

Ready for action with their camera and steel helmets are Lt. Ned R. Morehouse and Staff Sgt. Walter Emrich, both then of the 161st Signal Photographic Company, Fort Benning, Georgia. Lt. Morehouse directs the picture and Sgt. Emrich handled the newsreel camera. Captain Morehouse led the 196th Signal Photo Company as its commanding officer in Italy and former First Sergeant Emrich received a battlefield commission to second lieutenant.
—*Signal Corps Photo, SC 132163, National Archives*

Decoration and promotion ceremony of members of the 196th Signal Photo Co. Left to right: Maj. Linden G. Rigby, Army Pictorial Service Photo Officer, Fifth Army; 2nd Lt. Walter R. Emrich, Jr., (former First Sergeant), Tottenville, Staten Island, New York, Staff Sgt. Robert G. Edwards, Ashland, Ohio received Bronze Star; Pfc. Clarence E. Speicer, Corapolis, Pennsylvania, received Silver Star; First Sergeant Charles C. Baker, Atlanta, Georgia, received Bronze Star; Sgt. Robert F. Tacey, Liberty, New York, received Air Medal; Pfc. Albert A. Hauser, Brooklyn, N.Y. received Combat Infantryman's Badge; and Pfc. Roland L. Bronson, New York City, NY received the Combat Infantryman's badge.
—*Photo by Donald Wiedenmayer, 196th Signal Photo Company 111-SC 241430, National Archives*

Chapter 5

"Colonel Vosbergh" was here

Burke, John Mason and their driver, Snuffy Owens leave the city of Florence and travel to the city of Empoli, twenty miles to the west. Once in Empoli, Burke and John elect to leave their driver, Owens behind and drive off in their jeep in the direction of the village of Colli Alti, where Tina's family home, the Villa Calamai is located. They hope that a hand-drawn map Tina Calamai has given them will be sufficient to find their way, and upon their return to Florence, hope to be able to tell her that her immediate relatives, who now remain sheltered in the villa are safe.

After a few days, John and I were assigned to follow a company of South African troops who had been shifted to the western operations area near Florence and were traveling towards the outskirts of the industrial city of Empoli, twenty miles west.

The city of Empoli, a prominent bottle-making center, lies in the Arno Valley in northern Tuscany along the road to Pisa.

The two of us agreed that combat action in our assigned sector was quiet. About all we could find to photograph were some Allied tanks trying to ford the Arno River, some still-silent artillery positions and plenty of empty, flattened Italian farmhouses.

We "liberated" some much-needed photo finishing supplies that morning from the helpful owner of a local photo store in Empoli which included some much-needed paper and chemicals for our improvised field photo-finishing lab. The local weather in the city worsened by mid-day and the skies overhead turned progressively overcast.

Local farmers described the change in weather as evidence of the Bufera di Ferragosto. I knew in my own modest Italian, the word "ferragosto" meant holiday, so what else came after, given with the steadily blackening skies overhead, must truly be bad.

John and I decided to pack up our cameras and load our gear into our jeep for the day due to the increasingly lousy weather, and decided our time would be best spent by going to collect some Army food rations which could be found somewhere nearby in San Casciano. Within the picturesque Tuscan city of San Casciano, parts of its 14th century medieval city walls and towers still survive. The region later became known after the war for producing some of the most famous wines in the world.

Our driver, Snuffy Owens decided to sit out the storm in the company of local farmers until we could eventually return for him. The two of us set out our jeep early in the afternoon in the midst of a driving rain in the direction of where we remembered we had driven past a supply company's roadside field food ration dump.

I was at the wheel while John was busy looking at Tina's hastily-drawn map. Our reliable jeep continued to nimbly maneuver its way along the muddy roadway, puddle by puddle.

John looked up through the rain to regain his sense of direction.

"Hey look, Burke, aren't we heading in the direction where Tina's villa in Colli Alti is located?"

I asked him that we stop our jeep by the side of the road to give each of us a better look at the map.

I took out Tina's small penciled map I'd kept tucked in my shirt pocket for safekeeping since I last saw her in Florence and compared her drawing to the more official Italian road map I had obtained that day in the city of Empoli.

Tina's family villa, the Villa Calamai, certainly seemed to be in the same general geographical area we now found ourselves traveling but was situated on the opposite side of the Arno River from where we now were.

I didn't think John and I faced much difficulty in making sufficient time to take a brief detour from our primary purpose that day to find food rations for ourselves to properly pay the current occupants of the Villa Calamai a visit.

The road we were then traveling paralleled the Arno River and we simply needed a stroke of good luck to find a location to cross.

We started up our jeep and continued our journey looking for any sign of a possible bridgehead where we could cross.

Within about a mile or two, we sighted a slow moving, steady stream of vehicles of an American supply truck convoy. The motor sergeant in charge yelled back to us that his engineers had strung a Bailey bridge across the Arno River for safe use by light military vehicles not far from our position.

John and I followed the convoy for a few miles further and found the bridge the motor sergeant had described that was bobbing unsteadily up and down the now swelling Arno River.

We high-tailed it safely across the bridge with our jeep with measured sighs of relief and backtracked upstream along the road running parallel to the river until we found ourselves on a needed cross-road leading from the village of Signa.

A helpful Tuscan farmer pointed us in the direction of Colli Alti, the village situated immediately in front of the Villa Calamai.

When we felt that we had gone far enough towards Colli Alti, we asked another local farmer in our best Italian, "Dove Villa Calamai?" Italian villas were originally named after the family's surname.

The farmer drew his straggly arm from under his poncho and pointed to an iron gate about thirty yards ahead of us.

I was preparing to make a wide turn with our jeep to drive into the open villa's outer gate when the whole place became immediately alive with the deafening roar of incoming German artillery shells, and responding rounds quickly going out in reply.

The steady concussion of incoming shells were now hitting inside and behind the village of Colli Alti.

I floor-boarded the jeep through the gate, up the gravel driveway and skidded to a stop just beside the villa's vegetable garden.

Repeated salvos of outbound British 25-pound artillery shells not twenty yards away from me quickly answered the incoming German fire in near unison. John and I hastily made it from our jeep through a large half-opened heavy doorway towards safety.

So this was Tina's villa. It was one hell of a welcome John and I hadn't planned on.

A young British Army major came towards us clicking his boot heels along almost as soon as we were inside.

"Did you chaps draw all that fire?"

"If we did, then the Germans have a lot of ammo to waste. The Krauts could have just been clearing their pieces, too."

I was joking, but the British commander took my remarks rather seriously.

"I'd reckon not. Not with that many rounds."

He cupped his arms behind his back stiffly as the English tended to do when I sensed they felt a bit uptight when dealing with a Yank.

"Now, what's your business here, may I ask?"

I told the British major why John and I had chosen to pay the Villa Calamai a visit. We asked our congenial British host for his permission to speak to the Italian residents of the villa and to see about their personal safety.

He didn't seem especially helpful.

"I'm sorry, lads, but that's quite impossible. This is a military installation and under my command. I just cannot allow you to just roam the premises."

His bushy, fiery red eyebrows twitched with his every word.

I then tried a much different diplomatic approach. I undid my breast shirt pocket and took out Tina's handwritten note and also my official U.S. Army combat photographer's pass.

"Major, this is also the family residence of some people we met in Florence. They have people here who worked for them. They are naturally concerned for their safety, as well as the condition of this house. We intend to ascertain only that."

I handed him my official Army photographer's pass for his personal inspection.

"As for this military installation, this pass is signed by your own Field Marshal Harold Alexander himself of Allied Forces Headquarters (AFHQ) which officially permits us to roam wherever we may like."

AFHQ was the command headquarters that controlled all Allied operational forces in the Mediterranean Theatre of World War II from late 1942 to the end of the war.

The 15th Army Group was the highest command in Italy and commanded the Fifth US Army and 8th British Army. General Mark Clark was promoted to command the Group late in 1944.

It was just this sort of respectful, firm and uniquely American approach to doing business that endeared us affectionately to the hearts of our French and the English allies alike.

I had the distinct feeling that our Allies never quite liked those pesky Americans for intruding on what they thought was their own private war until they really needed us and had no choice.

The British major crisply handed my photographer's pass back to me.

"Yes, there are some Italians back there in the villa, through these doors.

Follow me."

John and I walked down a series of darkened corridors and passed through a series of heavy oak doors leading towards the kitchen.

The continuing roar sound of outgoing British artillery shells shook the ancient stone of the villa and heavy chunks of crumbling white plaster fell from the ceiling to the floor.

I cautiously opened a door and stepped down a small set of stone stairs which led into a lower storage type room, some three feet lower than the kitchen.

Cowering in a corner stood three much older Italian women, their heads covered with snug black scarves, their worn faces visibly terrified from fear.

Each kept chanting at one another in such rapid-fire Italian and held on tightly to their rosary beads as if they were waiting for what would soon be the end of their world.

The sudden physical presence of two large American soldiers must have also added to their immediate fear and concern. John and I towered above these Italian women on the stone steps, me standing at 6'3", and John somewhat smaller. Each of us wore dirty, dented steel Army field helmets on our heads and our faces were dirty and unshaven. We also wore .45 automatic pistols which hung from our khaki web belts.

I eased Tina's note from my outside pocket and with a measure of my own best broken Italian, softly asked, "Chi e Beppa?"

None of these older women acknowledged being Beppa, the family cook and helper Tina had asked us to befriend if we could.

As our words echoed through the room, one woman threw her hands in the air and fell to her knees before us moaning, "Oh Dio, no, Dio no."

The others soon chanted a litany and were of little help.

John looked at me, stupefied.

"These women are nuts. They think we are going to shoot them."

Our words fell on deaf ears.

We discovered it would be a few days before the two of us were able to travel back to Florence to share with Tina what little we had learned.

When the two of us eventually had a chance some days later to return to see our recent Florentine friends, Tina told us even if its occupants could not understand us, she herself was greatly relieved to find that everyone and everything at the villa was safe and sound.

Tina wasn't so much as thinking of herself, but was thinking of her father's general safety.

The most important material possessions her father, Signore Raffaello still had after so many years of cultivating the nearby land remained safely hidden deep within the villa's walls and any possible future income from the farms which surrounded it which could again produce once the fighting had ended.

Whatever modest amount of Italian lira that remained in the local banks had long ago lost its buying power as scarce food and goods grew steadily unaffordable as the war continued.

Tina said her father, Signore Raffaello, preferred to describe himself to be a simple man of the land whose entire life reflected a life in agriculture.

His agricultural expertise in winemaking was also valued and sought out throughout the region. Signore Raffaello also traveled outside Florence on business to offer much appreciated advice to wine makers in the southern part of France.

I admired Tina's sincere faith in the future. No matter what happened, she faithfully believed that their rich farmland land and the villa itself would always manage to survive.

Italian farmers, including her father, would need time to nourish their soil and recover from the ravages of war. With great joy, all members of this fabulous Calamai family had stood proudly together as if the war had already ended and their lives would begin once more.

Sooner or later, hopefully sooner, they would all reunite again under the same roof.

The immediate Calamai family had lived there in the villa in the village of Colli Alti, many of them, since a very early age. It was the local custom for agricultural families to entrust their young children to well-to-do families in order that they might be offered a secure life while going to school and learning the fine arts of cooking, sewing and homemaking.

These village people also became a part of the Calamai family circle and were cared for just as if they were blood relations.

All the young and old had worked under the skillful eye of Tina's mother, who had died before the war years.

Her mother came from San Sepolero in South Tuscany, well known for its gastronomic art. It was here, in San Sepolero that the famous house of Buitoni pasta was founded by schoolmates of Tina's mother. Guilia Buitoni, widow and mother of five children, pawned her jewelry to start the very first pasta factory in Italy in 1827.

Generations of family members found employment in villas like those owned by the Calamai family, or in similar family homes throughout the agricultural Tuscan region, while serving an apprenticeship. For when they decided to leave and get married or go on to be chefs in restaurants, as it happened many times, they were well-equipped to go out into the world with a preparation that held them well above the level of others.

My own lady luck, who had been doing so handsomely by guiding my destination during the war years, now gave me a special wave of her magic wand to set matters so perfectly in place that it couldn't have been done better if a genie had given me three wishes.

A large historic villa, especially one as grand in size as Tina's family home, resting comfortably out in the country near Florence, was a ready military target for both sides.

The villa served as a convenient rest stop for American combat troops moving through the area, and secondly, for local villagers needing a protective place to squat and better their home life positions.

John and I were briefed by our operations officer at 3131st Signal Service Battalion headquarters one morning when we learned that the South African troops in our sector would be moving from their positions above Empoli to the Florence-Pistoia road which ran into the Apennine Mountains.

This upcoming troop movement meant that the British and South African forces they had earlier encountered at the villa would now be gone, and it's the family could now safely return.

I couldn't believe my eyes. I looked at the map and quickly noticed how the little village of Colli Alti, where Tina's villa was located, was only one mile from the main road near our own Fifth Army lines.

It was hard to hold back my enthusiasm.

John smiled and looked at me.

"Burke, it might be hard to find a good place to bed down around there; don't you think?"

I eagerly agreed.

"In that case, John, we might as well move before the mad rush begins. I think I might know of a place that might be perfect."

When I was in the port of Naples, I came to know an Army major at Allied headquarters who was Italian-American by birth. John and I once needed a set of four tires for a little Fiat Topolino we had acquired as a military means for private travel.

This major handed us a batch of U.S. Army supply requisition forms officially signed by a "Colonel H. Vosbergh, U.S. Army, Commanding," which had been printed by the hundreds.

His instructions to us sounded simple enough.

"Just fill in what you want, boys, and sign them. Then tell who ever you hand them to, Mussolini or whoever is in charge they will pay the bill after the war."

The forms looked too good to be true, so John and I eagerly scooped up a handful and decided we would put them to the test whenever we needed to requisition much-needed supplies.

We brought one of these official forms with us on our next trip to the Villa Calamai. While John parked our jeep, I took one of these very same official supply requisition forms and duly filled it out and tacked it to the front door of the Villa Calamai.

"John, welcome home," I said triumphantly.

He seemed a little unconvinced. "Do you think it's legal?"

"John, it's always worked. The only time I ever got outranked was when Henry Cabot Lodge, Jr. and company made me move from the villa I once occupied in Naples."

Lodge had quit the U.S. Senate from Massachusetts to serve as an Army lieutenant colonel at the start of the war.

I didn't take my eviction by such a high-ranking former U.S. senator all that personally.

"Besides, look at that official signature.

Colonel H. Vosbergh, U.S. Army, Commanding."

By the end of the Italian Campaign, through our help, our very special generous Army benefactor, the fictitious "Colonel Vosbergh" got around to just about as many places in Italy as the ever-popular Kilroy.

Chapter 6

Rebirth of the Villa Calamai

Tina Calamai and her friend Rina make an eight-mile bicycle trip from Florence to return to their family home, the Villa Calamai, where Burke O'Connell and his partner, John Mason have now established temporary living quarters. Secret rooms open to reveal the historic Medici villa's hidden treasures safely kept out of the hands of both their German and Italian fascist occupiers. O'Connell is delighted to learn more about Tina and her family, and finds his attraction to her beginning to grow.

The day after John and I moved into the Villa Calamai, Tina and Rina came out to join us from nearby Florence on their bicycles. The one-way journey was about an eight-mile trip, but these two sturdy young women completed the round trip so many times before while they each were living in the Villa Calamai they hardly looked tired when they arrived.

Lucia, the villa's housemaid of some twenty years, had arrived the day before and had begun to organize local farmers' womenfolk into individual teams of cleaning, dusting and generally putting the villa back into proper order after the passage of so many soldiers of all sides.

From secret rooms hidden deep within the villa's kitchen and from a deep underground room beneath the outside garden, all kinds of things began to come out of their hiding places.

John and I found it unbelievable how much the Germans had overlooked or could not find during their occupation. The entire Medici family would have been proud, too, that their secrecy, for which they had a penchant, had been put to such good use.

The two-story villa remains a large, rectangular-shaped structure with large windows, corniced in a grey stone, that the ground floor was laced with heavy iron grills that afforded the level of protection so desired by the affluent families of the Renaissance era. The massive structure had been built by the Medici family around 1550 as a hunting lodge for their large palatial villa at Poggio a Caiano some three miles away.

The doors that led into the main garden were large, cathedral type, constructed in heavy oak that must have been twenty feet high. The downstairs rooms were immense, with heavy beamed oak ceilings characteristic of Tuscan country villas of the period.

A measure of serenity had generally returned to the immediate area around the villa. Traces of war could only be found in passing Army truck convoys and the far distant rumble of artillery.

Having accomplished all that they considered impossible on their very first day back at the villa, Tina, Rina and Lucia returned to Florence with one of the village farmers in a large two-wheeled wagon pulled by ever-faithful Nello, an older white-spotted horse with a bobbed tail. Tina had told me how family members fashioned a false tail that fitted over Nello's stub so that he could shoo away the flies.

The three women would later return with Tina's father, Signore Raffaello, and all the belongings they had taken during their temporary evacuation to Florence.

Much work remained to be done to bring a measure of order and comfort back to the villa. Early first steps had been taken, but there was more important hard work to follow.

John and I watched as all kinds of household goods, foodstuffs and metal utensils literally came out of the woodwork. From all types of secret compartments that had been carefully plastered over at the start of the war came containers of olive oil, wine, pasta and copper pans that had escaped Mussolini's war appropriation of precious metals.

Stacks of family dishes and all sorts of silverware would appear almost daily from their secret hiding places. The most ingenious hiding places were yet to be revealed, and in their exposure to freedom from German and Italian tyranny came the very real salvation of the entire Calamai family in the very lean postwar months that followed.

The villa had been a traditional hub of community agricultural agency with several nearby highly productive farms situated in the village of Colli Alti closely around it. All equipment and storage was maintained here. All the grapes were gathered in and brought to this central cellar for wine making. In one large cellar room, there were eight enormous oval casks, some twenty-five feet high.

It was within these same oval casks that the mashed grapes were first allowed to ferment before being taken to a much lower and cooler cellar for the final stage of winemaking. As the war went steadily sour for Italy, the grapes did likewise, due largely in part to lack of hand care that the vines typically required, to say nothing of the necessary pesticides that were by now non-existent.

The majority of the winemaking casks in the villa had been empty for most of the time, and they were cleverly put to profitable use as strategic hiding places.

Under the villa's heavy stone floor, just below the line of oval vats, the original Medici's had also seen fit to build large and very dry rooms, constructed entirely out of brick.

These rooms were discovered quite by accident by later family members only a few years prior to the start of the war.

Each individual wine vat had a large manhole in the end for raking out the grape hulls when the first free run of wine was completed.

Inside the vat, when the staves were dry, one could pry up three large staves making the bottom of the vat accessible from below. While still inside the vat, a large stone could be pried up and below it, leading to a secret room in waiting. The Calamai family had stored all imaginable things within in these rooms.

When the possibility of confiscation, first from the Italians, then the Germans, became evident, they had stored wheat in glass demijohns, olive oil, tomato paste, silver, linens, blankets, heirloom paintings and anything of personal value that would strike the eye of any passing enemy military or Italian fascist official who sought to come by with a license to steal under official government authority.

I guess old Tina's father, Signore Raffaello Calamai genuinely knew what he was talking about when he said the rich lands of his Italian homeland would never betray him.

Early one morning as John and I prepared to "go to war" as Tina's father described each of us, we were greeted by a handsome young South African infantry sergeant outside the villa's gate who said his unit had secured a generous supply of available fresh water and he wanted to know if it was okay with our Colonel Vosbergh if they installed a complete shower and laundry facility immediately nearby.

John and I could hardly believe our luck. Before either one of us could speak, John beat me to it.

"What you're telling us sergeant, is that you want to install hot and cold running showers?"

He turned his sly face toward me.

"I think that could be arranged, don't you?"

I enthusiastically agreed, and firmly shook the South African sergeant's hand. Before we were finished with our business, I wanted know if the residents of the villa could use the facility as well.

"If not the showers, could they have at least all the hot water they wanted?"

The South African chap was unusually cooperative.

"Oh, it's no trouble at all, and if you want, 1 can run a rubber hose over to their kitchen."

John and I each agreed that our South African ally offered us an incredible deal and the prospect of no longer having to heat water over a Coleman stove began to really hit home.

I was certain too, that Beppa, the family cook, would be especially happy to have hot water in the villa's kitchen once again.

So with the villa's plumbing situation now satisfactorily resolved, John and I went happily off to our war which was waiting for us not too many miles away.

Our driver, Snuffy Owens, summed up the situation by saying, "Hell, this beats the post showers back at Fort Bragg."

We also recalled the misery of army basic training and the lengthy walk to the showers which always seemed to be filled up.

Not far from the Villa Calamai, the three of us discovered one of the Army's mobile doughnut units operated by Millie Proudfoot of the American Red Cross which had been thoughtfully set up by the intersection of the Signa-Pistoia road.

Millie was a tall, lanky college-age Vassar girl who had the habit of showing up with her doughnut machine in the damnedest places to "dispense doughnuts to our boys and a little cheer."

Our driver, Snuffy, began putting them away, two doughnuts at a time.

Who would have believed it?

Fresh, hot, tasty doughnuts right here in the middle of a damn war.

John gave Snuffy a playful poke in his ribs.

"Snuff, stick with us, and you'll wear diamonds on your Army Good Conduct Medal."

Mason shoved his hand warmly across the counter.

"Millie, God bless you, you've really made our day. See you tomorrow. And you can take it from this soldier, Honest John Mason; you're making this one hell of a war."

You often felt an immediate eerie feeling when you entered a newly liberated small town for the first time. You had the unavoidable anxious feeling that there was always someone watching you from some hidden vantage point.

John and I shared that level of uneasiness when we entered the outskirts of Pistoia for the first time.

The town, medieval in every aspect, is situated at the foot of the massive cliffs of the Apennine Mountains.

A German rear guard was known to operate around the town, sniping and harassing Allied soldiers and local citizens alike. A substantial group of Italian partisans continued to engage in fire fights with German infantry believed to be entrenched in the nearby cemetery.

John and I found the village of Pistoia largely deserted and you could cut the general quietness in the air with a sharp knife. The sudden explosion of mortar shells, either ours or theirs in the outskirts of town broke the silence.

In Pistoia, the two of us took our still photo equipment over to a community square to take some casual pictures of various historical landmarks and a beautiful frieze in Della Robbia terra cotta across the pillars of one of the buildings.

While I stood outside, John went inside one of the structures to take a closer look. I finished my filming and got into the driver's seat of our jeep and started the motor.

I discovered that keeping the motor running was a critical precaution that in combat could save your life.

When John walked out of the building, the two of us heard the sounds of another motor not that far in the distance. John took his seat in the jeep and we hesitatingly sat still for one last moment trying to make out what type of vehicle was approaching us before making our getaway.

A German Volkswagen military jeep came into view with what looked like a pair of well-dressed Germans in civilian dress inside. We could see these two men were not combat soldiers and we knew we couldn't get out of there without crossing their path on the opposite side of the piazza. So John and I decided to play a waiting game.

It was impossible that the Germans didn't see us, or maybe at this moment, they didn't want to.

After to us what seemed like an eternity, the weathered German VW reached the end of the piazza and turned out of our line of sight.

John quickly told me to hit the gas of our jeep and to get us the hell out of there.

I zinged my way across the piazza and rapidly out of the town. We noticed no one behind us, and heard the occasional sound in the distance of falling mortar rounds.

We returned to the safety and comfort of the villa.

One night, Tina asked me if we could meet for lunch the next day. Some of the friends that we had met in Florence were coming out to the villa and her husband would also be there.

I couldn't quite understand why I should meet Tina's husband, but the general idea did not seem unpleasant to me.

While Tina appealed to me very much, we had not gone beyond the stage of holding hands, some close dancing, and the exchange of a modest kiss.

Since our driver, Snuffy had been saying that the jeep needed some overdue maintenance I thought the upcoming luncheon date could not be any better.

So, it was maintenance for the jeep and a luncheon date for Tina and I.

Lunch the following day turned out to be a real journey through the Italian culinary arts of Beppa, a delightful paradox of a woman, whose general appearance looked more gypsy than Florentine. Her hair was long, black and wiry, and she kept it tightly covered and neatly arranged with a colorful silk scarf.

She had an interesting face, similar to one that Cezanne might have painted. Here was this peasant of peasants, with clubby hands and a crooked face, turning out dishes that could easily turn the heads of the most discriminating gourmets anywhere in the world.

The left side of Beppa's face was slightly paralyzed, which made her mouth move upward as she thoughtfully spoke in melodic Italian. The overall, positive effect made her appear to always smile when she talked.

Not only was each dish deliciously prepared, but each was carefully presented on an infinite number of platters and dishes in a manner that would do justice to a double spread in *House and Gardens* magazine.

Tina's mother had molded Beppa from a young, bashful country girl into a highly sophisticated cook who would blush with embarrassment over any compliment on one of her dishes.

Of course, little Lucia did the dishes justice and carried them in grand style as she served each guest. It was amazing how these people, with such simple beginnings, could carry off their tasks in a manner that would please any family in the highest of society.

Since the family had arrived at the villa, we had not seen too much of Tina's father, Signore Raffaello, other than a discreet greeting of "buon giorno" or "buona notte."

At the lunch, Signore Raffaello sat at the head of the table and looked approvingly at each dish that was brought before him.

Sadly, all he could do was look lovingly at each attractive dish since diabetes forced him to stay on a highly restricted diet.

I say forced, because that was the only way the proud Italian gentleman would adhere to it. He had been a gourmet and wine expert all his life and now, even though he could not partake of the foods prepared, he still liked the ritual of refusal as Lucia would pass each platter in front of him.

He would stare thoughtfully at each dish, as though deciding whether or not to take it, and with a wave of his hand, dismiss the whole idea. Sometimes, when Tina would not be looking, he would stick in a quick fork and grab a bite.

At this moment, Lucia would pretend to be looking the other way, and would have to cover her mouth so as not to show her smile.

Signore Raffaello was a kindly man with a broad face, ruddy from the outdoor life he had always led. He said he came from an extended family of textile people and much to his father's dislike, he decided to attend college to study agriculture rather than enter business.

His brothers made a considerable fortune with a process for regenerating wool from rags and flooding the Middle East markets with their products. But as the war clouds steadily gathered, shipping and international commerce came to a virtual standstill; it was the rebellious farmer brother who fed them while their merchandise stacked high in warehouses.

The lunch ended late in the afternoon, as is the custom with most Italian luncheons, or even dinners, for that matter.

We were gathered outside in the villa garden swapping handshakes.

Giuglio, Tina's husband, had his Lancia parked there. It was a long, black luxurious four-door sedan. If someone asked me to describe Giuglio, I think I would have to say that he was the sort of guy who happily drove a Lancia while the rest of Florence went by bicycles or on foot.

And when the Allied Military Group (AMG) went looking for a local distributor for flour, rice or other essentials, whom do you think they decided to pick?

They naturally picked Giuglio, of course.

True, he had always been in that business and the AMG probably felt it would be the simplest way to get the food to the local people.

The pleasant situation was also the simplest way for a man like him to make a fortune by dividing these important supplies to pasta factories, restaurants and bakeries.

The Allies always seemed to have a knack for picking the wrong people.

Later on, John and Rina went for a bicycle ride while Tina and I went for a walk in the meadow with her faithful dog, Giovacchino, a Scotch setter, tagging alongside.

As we walked along, Tina turned to me and said, "You know, Giuglio really liked you."

I was curious why.

"Tell me something. Why did you want me at that lunch? Was it just to meet him?"

"I told him about you and John taking occupation of the villa. He immediately had a picture in his mind of the typical American soldier and probably thought I might also have some interest. You see, as I said, he's more possessive than jealous. I wanted him to see how fine and good looking you truly are."

So what was her motive? I had to know.

"Then you weren't using me to get back at him?"

"No, I'm not vindictive. What was between us stopped a long time ago. This way he can think what he wants and it will save a lot of useless explanations."

I soon found myself taking both her hands into mine as I looked deeply into her eyes.

"Did anyone ever tell you that your eyes are every bit as attractive as actress Tallulah Bankhead's?"

"Just who is Tallulah Bankhead?"

Another more recent popular American movie star, due to Mussolini's embargo on all things American that Tina didn't know.

"Forget it." I leaned closer to her lips and she slipped her arms around my neck.

I pulled her tender lips onto mine and closed my eyes.

The air swirling about the bright green meadow tasted as fresh and clean as the first moments after an afternoon rain. Her dog, Giovacchino, looked up at us approvingly from a sunny spot on the grass.

All of a sudden, the meadow seemed the most beautiful place in the world. We were caught up in a rapture of romantic attraction that swirled all around us.

We were falling into the grasp of love as we clung closer and closer to one another with each moment.

Later that evening, we sat before the fireplace drinking glasses of some fine French cognac that Giuglio had given to Tina before for a persistent toothache.

The cognac was better enjoyed by the four of us seated before the huge fireplace, watching the evening fire eat the logs one by one.

John lowered the needle of the family phonograph to play a favorite and familiar recording of Bing Crosby singing "September Song." The song's gentle lyrics fit the mood and the moment so very well.

Autumn weather had come and turned the leaves to colorful flames.

We knew our days together had dwindled down to a similar precious few before John and I would be off to the front lines once more.

"And these few precious days
I spend with you.
These precious days
I spend with you."

Ours had been a memorable day and the evening we had spent together was just as beautiful. The war seemed a million miles away.

Lucia, the friendly family maid, came in with some small ceramic pots and began filling them with red hot ashes from the fire. I couldn't understand what she was doing.

Tina saw the look of curiosity in my eyes as she asked, "Haven't you ever seen the fire in the bed?"

I struggled to understand what she meant.

"The fire in the bed; you must be kidding."

The four of us then accompanied Lucia upstairs with the pots on a carrying stick that had hooks for five pots. They put a wooden frame, made in a sort of oval shape, inside the bedcovers so that they stayed raised up from the mattress. The hot air could then circulate inside the raised bedcovers. This process was done two or sometimes three hours before going to bed. Since the villa was without any heat other than fireplaces, the bedrooms tended to be not only very cold, but damp.

Our Army-issued sleeping bags did not offer John and I very much in the way of comfort or real warmth when we slept outdoors on hard, cold ground.

A few generous swigs of strong cognac often helped warm us up and cut the fall chill before we turned in for the night.

The next day, John and I had a message waiting for us at the 3131st Signal Service Battalion operations tent. It seemed that they wanted a full cover story on the city of Pisa since, to that date, only token random photographs by Allied combat photographers had been taken.

Pisa had been placed off-limits and all the entrances to it were closed off with barbed wire and protected from looting by U.S. Army MPs.

The official command reasoning in this case made real sense, and had it been done in earlier instances, there would be healthier American GI's walking around with both hands and arms.

The people of Pisa quickly evacuated the city almost en masse, leaving their personal belongings in their homes and their goods in their stores.

The Germans then came along and what they didn't take, they cleverly booby-trapped for Allied troops to find.

The city of Pisa compares in size to San Diego, California, and to see a metropolitan area completely cordoned off, isolated from everything and with not a living soul in it, produced a strangeness the likes of which I had never experienced before.

In smaller villages, you expected the eerie quiet.

But walking through the streets of Pisa felt like being in a set in a surreal science fiction film.

The weather in Pisa was overcast, and we had felt rain on and off since we arrived. A slight, but constant wind stirred the shallow puddles of water that filled the barren streetscape.

Every now and then, we would hear the scratchy metallic sound of a rusty sign beating against a building, or a loose metal store shutter which would make a long, creaking noise that made you immediately turn and look back. You felt at any moment, some ancient figure would step out of the shadows and point a threatening finger at the invaders patrolling the empty streets of the city.

Without knowing where we were going or even how to get there, we came into a large piazza that took our breath away.

John looked up and exclaimed, "Christ, Burke, it's the Leaning Tower of Pisa!"

We somehow did not expect to be coming down a narrow street and then, bingo, see the famous Leaning Tower before our eyes.

Usually you get this sort of thing gradually. We sat in the jeep just looking at the whole spectacle of the piazza. It was an incredible feeling; having the whole view to ourselves. It was like it was all ours.

The whole thing, the Baptistery, the Cathedral and the Tower itself, leaning like nothing I had ever seen before, yet strong and sturdy.

How could it be possible, with all the destruction that had happened around the immediate area, all the bombs that fell, destroying the outskirts of the city that the famous Tower of Pisa could still be leaning there undamaged, in defiance?

I thought truly, they really knew what they were doing when they named the piazza. It surely was a 'Piazza of Miracles.'

Late that same afternoon, we passed by headquarters to leave off our film for the courier. There was another message there for us. It said that we were to report the following day to Army Pictorial Service, Fifth Army Headquarters for assignment towards the front lines.

That meant that life at the villa was now finished for us. The war's brutal reality was far away from the Villa Calamai. It had moved to the cold, muddy fields atop the Apennine Mountains.

John and I drove back to the villa in silence.

We did have a good laugh at the table while eating dinner.

Tina's father had asked her to ask us if we had seen the tower of Pisa and what we had thought of it.

I gave John a playful wink and told them that the famous tower was very impressive, but that it had been terribly damaged by the war and was still leaning very much. I assured them that they should not have any fears about it though because the Army Engineer Corps was busy right now straightening it up. In a couple of days, the Leaning Tower will be like new again.

Well, when this got translated, Tina, Rina and Signore Raffaello all went into hysterics. I guess they believed the Americans capable of just about anything.

John added to the commotion by saying, "the damn thing is dangerous leaning like that!"

I think after a while we raised the old man's blood pressure just a little too much. We did our best to set the story straight. Even as he went to bed, he still had to be reassured again that the American engineers didn't straighten the Tower.

Later on, Tina asked me to accompany her upstairs to stir up the fire in the bed. So we took an oil lamp and went up.

She stirred the fire in Rina's room and then in her room. After she did, she came toward me.

I took her in my arms and kissed her, almost desperately. "Tina," I said, gazing deeply in her brilliant eyes, "I want you very much."

Her eyes fixed on mine. "And I want you, too."

"There's something I must tell you. We got some orders today. We have to leave here, tomorrow. Early."

Her eyes swelled up with tears as she asked, "Where to? Will you be far away?"

"Far enough, I guess, in Monghidoro. Do you know where that is?"

"Dio mio, that's almost to Bologna."

Tina's eyes searched mine for some quick, simple solution to the painful question. They searched mine for something that would make it not so absolute.

"I guess it is." I held her closer. "I'll tell you something. I promise you that I will come back. I can't say when, because I don't know. But I'll come back. Will you be here?"

"Do you mean at the village of Colli Alti?"

I nodded.

"If you say you will come back, I'll be here."

I kissed her and squeezed her and said, "I think I'd better take that fire out of the bed. We could get burned; what do you say?"

We undressed and slid into the bed together.

When our bodies touched between the hot sheets, a wave of sensuous excitement swept over me. I held Tina close to me and I could feel within my heart something she had been deprived of and now longing for even more.

Little by little, the oil lamp, wishing to be discreet, slowly dimmed itself.

I knew that this precious moment, one I never expected to happen to me during the course of the war, was actually happening for real, and there was absolutely nothing I could do to stop it.

There was nothing Tina could do about it either.

We had stepped on the land where the earth was loose.

We were sinking down in its grip.

We were falling in love with all sincerity, but also desperately and perhaps, hopelessly.

And I didn't want to stop.

Chapter 7

A special photo assignment

The U.S. Fifth Army concentrated its primary attack during the month of October 1944 along Highway 65 north leading towards the city of Bologna.

The Germans fell back through a series of defensive positions including the Monghidoro, Loiano and Livergnano lines inflicting heavy losses for each mile of the Allied advance.

Our boss, Major Linden Rigby at 3131st Signal Service Company gave John Mason and I a welcome early Christmas present in the form of a plum photo assignment far away from the front lines.

This assignment would take several weeks to complete while providing photographic coverage of an important gasoline fuel pipeline then being from Leghorn south of Florence towards our current front lines.

The Allied fall 1944 offensive towards Bologna, which began with much promise, soon bogged down under worsening weather and tough German resistance by the end of the month and did not advance much farther than Livergnano by its end.

John and I thought we had been clever sneaking off in the dead of night from the field throughout the month of September 1944 to return to the Villa Calamai as often as possible without Major Rigby's knowledge.

We would now be farther from his official supervision during the assignment and have a real reason to use the villa as a much-preferred base of operations.

Army engineers had been busy building a four-inch double gasoline pipeline which ran from the Standard Oil pumping station in the port of Leghorn all the way across half of Tuscany and up the Apennine mountains.

Gasoline was soon dispensed at the front lines just like at a typical filling station back in the States, but without the added full-service touch of cleaning your windshield and checking your oil. Construction of this line started soon after Fifth Army captured the critical port of Leghorn on July 19, 1944 in August 1944, near Livorno.

When Fifth U.S. Army captured Leghorn, they found it in ruins. The Germans, who occupied the port, had erected barricades, blown bridges, laid mines, and sunk twenty ships to completely seal off the harbor entrances. For their part, in some 50 raids during the first half of 1944, the Allies had dropped more than 1,000 tons of bombs.

John and I would also film the ongoing activities of Army pipeline walkers tasked to inspect the lines for damage and the construction of several individual booster pumping stations then being completed.

Rigby seemed genuinely proud that he was also offering us an assignment tailor made for the two of us. I think honestly looking back; Major Rigby was a nicer guy than we often gave him credit for.

The Villa Calamai was about a 45-minute drive by jeep from the port of Leghorn where our primary photographic coverage would begin. The scope of the project was a great engineering achievement and certainly laid the groundwork for the oil pipelines that were built in the Middle East soon after the war.

While American engineers rebuilt shipping berths, British naval demolition teams continued opening the harbor. Berths for six Liberty ships soon gave Leghorn a capacity to handle 12,000 tons of vital supplies per day by the end of September 1944.

So the Villa Calamai once again became our home for the duration of this photo assignment.

I sensed this time Tina began to feel it was to be an almost permanent thing. It just did not seem destined that we would ever be very far away. The funny thing about all of this was that I was beginning to believe it myself.

Sometimes we were working very close to the Villa Calamai since the pipeline at one point ran about three miles away near the village of Signa. So, Tina and I had time during the month of September to spend together. We took bicycle rides with John and Rina and had picnic sandwiches with wine along the meadows where local hunters were always looking out for some unsuspecting birds. We would go wild mushroom hunting in the hills above Carmingnana and sat for hours before the villa's fireplace listening to phonograph records.

Late one night, Tina discreetly told me that before she knew me she had lost all interest in physical intimacy. She thought that she had become frigid. Her life with her husband had so turned her off to men that at one point she even thought of going into a convent. Her mother's brother was a Franciscan priest. Tina told me she had hoped to have children one day, but her husband had become sterile due to a long untreated venereal disease. This, coupled with the humiliation of his past blatant infidelity, made her personal life, she said, rather miserable.

She put her life into painting and skiing which were the only two things that she cared about. Her deep affection for her mother was dealt a harsh blow when she died abruptly just as she was preparing to leave the hospital after a simple operation. Then the war came and life became more and more difficult. She divided her time between her two houses. Her life became a routine existence. She suffered a life without scope, satisfaction or reward. To face that period without the aid and comfort of someone who really cared for her was a sorrowful task.

Then one day, she was waiting for her best friend to come for lunch when there was an air raid in the near vicinity. Her friend called to tell her that she would be late because of the raid. She never arrived for lunch. They found her body under the rubble two days later.

Fortunately, her good friend, Rina, came for a visit, and as fate would have it, the war situation made it impossible to leave Florence. Tina always felt that some kind of providence had made this happen. Then I came along. It seemed to her that someone, somewhere, perhaps her mother who loved her dearly, wanted it all to happen. She was happy. This was an experience she had not felt for many years.

When we would lie in that warm bed, holding on to each other, we really felt that it was meant to be. It all happened so naturally. We refused to discuss what would come later. We knew nothing of the future. We had made a conquest of the present, but even if we didn't speak of it, we knew a future was ahead of us. A future we would share with each other when it became the present.

Chapter 8

Premonition

Loiano, Italy

John Mason and I finished our pipeline story by early November 1944 on the high flat ground on Highway 65, about thirty miles from Bologna.

It was an amazing engineering feat and one that everyone just took for granted. We had actually installed a filling station not more than eight miles from the front. We returned to our place in the Loiano farmhouse not realizing the tragic events that were to take place, bringing us grief and also bringing us to the point of ending our days on that mountain.

The Germans had a night fighter-bomber, probably a Junkers JU-88, which flies over our positions each evening at all different altitudes.

Several infantrymen of the 91st Infantry Division remarked that he was just checking to see if they were all present and accounted for. This plane earned the name of Bed Check Charlie. The German pilot would fly over the Monghidoro area usually about nine, midnight, and then about three a.m. His primary mission was harassment and observation of our forces and his antics kept all of us on the ground on edge.

His bombs were intended for our entrenched artillery positions or field headquarters but his aim in the past had not been too accurate, which became a fine point in our favor.

On the evening of November 12, 1944, John and I heard the sound of the same German Luftwaffe night bomber flying over us while we were in bed.

The droning sound of the aircraft sounded lower in the sky than usual. We soon heard the thunderous concussion of a bomb exploding close by but heard nothing further. The walls of the farmhouse shook a little, but that was all. We eventually drifted off to sleep.

Early the next morning, our driver Snuffy Owens drove John and I to Corps headquarters in Monghidoro to pick up more film and drop off our most recently exposed work for processing.

When we arrived in the village, Owens immediately noticed a considerable amount of activity concentrated around the ruins of a house along an s-bend in the road.

"Hey, ain't that Maxie's place?"

I looked up through the windshield of the jeep as we drew nearer to the scene.

"Sure looks like it," I said.

When we got to the area, we could see that a bomb had hit the house where Tech. Sgt. Max Campbell, 23, had bedded down that evening, along with fellow photographer, Tech. 4 Harry Morgan, 25, and their driver, Pvt. Nelson Pitts.

Soldiers could be seen actively clearing the smoldering rubble of the ruined stone farmhouse from the bombing the night before.

We watched as a hoist carefully lifted Campbell's battered body as it was skillfully hauled out from the wreckage, still encased in his Army sleeping bag. He resembled an ancient mummy covered in dense, white dust from head to toe. The Army medics who treated him gave Campbell a shot of morphine to ease his pain, but Max appeared to us to be in too bad of shape for that. I learned that he died a few hours later in a nearby field hospital. Morgan was also taken to the field hospital, but died from his wounds four days later on November 16, 1944. Their driver, Pitts luckily escaped serious injury.

Later on that same day, John and I and all other photo teams working in the area were called to our unit's field headquarters.

Everyone was noticeably upset ever Campbell's death. In a unit the size of ours, when anyone is wounded or suddenly killed in action, you quickly realize how vulnerable you can also become.

The driving distance between Max's house and our own was only two miles.

The immediate thought made me shudder, while at the same time I thought of Tina who could have lost me.

It was only two miles.

I wonder how such decisions are made in the "Big Command Post" high in the sky.

Who chooses whom?

I had always felt that I had been especially blessed during the war. What I wanted now was to continue to keep holding on to that luck until the war finally came to an end.

But then, I knew Max Campbell had been lucky before. Campbell, 23, from Mesa, Arizona, had recorded action at Kasserine Pass, El Guettar and Gafsa in Tunisia. He and his newsreel camera also jumped with the 82nd Airborne Division in Sicily. He was the only cameraman to go in with the amphibious assault behind the German lines at Santa Agata in Sicily and saw action at Monte Cassino and Anzio.

Sometimes you just have to you ask yourself, how lucky can you get?

How much of life's precious time are you allotted?

Rigby was visibly upset by what had happened, and said to all of us, he felt, as most field commanders would, that something had to be done to assure the general safety of all personnel who reported to him.

He immediately ordered that still and motion picture photographer teams currently located in a forward combat area would have to move behind a designated operations line to be assigned by Fifth Army headquarters.

John and I vigorously protested, saying that where we were was just as safe a place as any that could then be found along that already-dangerous stretch of Highway 65. Rigby would have no part of our concerns and ordered us back.

Enemy bombs or artillery do not discriminate their targets, and can drop on any place at any time.

Rigby's immediate solution to the problem was a typical Army response to the onset of a sudden crisis.

Since John and I were the unit's most forwardly located team, his order was directed at us. We were then located in Loiano, just north of Monghidoro.

"I want the both of you to move back today. Is that clear?"

Rigby wasn't one for mincing words.

"I don't want either of you to spend another night where you are."

We each nodded in agreement.

"You both are my responsibility, and I'm telling you to move back. There's no military necessity for either of you to be where you are."

"Yes, sir," we replied.

That was it.

There were no bucking official orders like that.

The major felt his decision to move us back would place us within an acceptable safety zone. What he did not then know, nor could we possibly suspect was that Rigby had actually placed us right on death's doorstep and would have blown the both of us to kingdom come.

What saved both our lives was nothing short of an absolute miracle, and I can now use that word in retrospect, quite certainly.

John and I decided to move our base of operations south from the village of Loiano to nearby La Rocca, close enough to the front lines, but still within the safety zone Rigby had required of us.

The tiny Italian village of La Rocca consisted of little more than a small cluster of old stone farm houses and a few small shops, situated along an s-curve on Highway 65, about five miles from Monghidoro where both Max Campbell and Morgan had recently lost their lives.

John and I found a single upstairs room in a small, two-story home of a forest guard named Rinaldo and his young wife, Assunta, who were the parents of a five-year-old boy and the owners of a large, affectionate, shaggy dog who lovingly adopted us.

Our sleeping quarters had a small window which gave us a modest view of the highway outside, and lacked heat.

John and I improvised a cook stove from a discarded 240 mm howitzer shell casing we recently recovered and soon had it working. The improvised stove used a fuel piping system which formed a sort of a generator when gasoline flowed into it. A small hole in the pipe permitted a modest flame that would heat the pipe situated above it. When the pipe grew hot, the liquid fuel would transform into a gas. This fuel mix could then be regulated by a small regulator knob. Our stove provided a considerable amount of heat, and in no time at all, our room was cozy warm. We didn't have to watch its daily fuel consumption since a gas station, located a few miles away to the rear of us, was now open for business.

One day while we were filling up our cans I asked the guy running the hose how the fuel line was working.

"It's terrific," he replied. "It's hard to think that this gas is coming all the way from . . . where is it?"

"Livorno," I told him.

"Yeah, like I said, it's coming all the way from Livorno. I just hope the Germans don't try and knock it out."

"They'll never do it," I replied. "To reach this far, they'd need a railroad gun."

The gasoline cans were soon filled and John and I left.

We returned to Rinaldo's two-story home. His wife was a young, dark girl from Sardinia. He said he was born in Corsica, but lived a long time in Sardinia where they first met.

He worked as a forest ranger performing patrol duty in the state-owned forest ranges. Much of his duties were performed at night, and he always took his big dog with him for company.

His wife was generally a good cook and we often ate with family downstairs while we lived there.

Rinaldo always had some good wine or potent grappa to offer us.

After dinner, John and I would go upstairs and sit around our stove and talk, tell jokes or read. Sometimes we would just play cards. Usually, the two of us each went to bed early.

We left La Rocca to take photographs of an awards ceremony near II Corps Headquarters. While I was filming the ceremony, I thought I heard my name being called. I looked around and saw there was no one around me. I heard my name being called again, but this time I identified the voice as Tina's.

I'm usually a skeptic when it comes to superstitious matters, but somehow, this voice was so clear that it frightened me. I kept thinking of it throughout the day.

John and I returned to La Rocca later that afternoon. We went upstairs and all three of us had a jolt of grappa. I sat on the cot and lit a cigarette before dinner.

John came over to me.

"Hey kid, what's got into you? Are you all right?"

It was the first indication that what I felt inside now showed up on my face.

I told John what had happened earlier.

"John, I just got the feeling that something's happening down there at the villa. I really believe that."

"Well, if it's worrying you, Burke, why don't we just take off this evening and go see?"

That was John.

Without changing clothes, we left our driver Snuffy there at Rinaldi's home, and just at twilight, took off for the Villa Calamai.

When we arrived at the villa, Tina and Rina were both especially anxious to see us. Our visit was not on one of the pre-appointed days, yet they did not seem too surprised to see us.

When I told Tina what I had experienced earlier that day, she told me that she and Rina had both felt that something had happened to John and I. Neither knew exactly what might have happened, but they just felt that something dangerous had suddenly befallen us.

We were all together once more, so there was no real reason to worry anymore, was there?

That was the end of the strange voices and weird thoughts in our heads. The spooky atmosphere we felt was quickly cleared with a couple of drinks and after that no one spoke any further of it before going to bed.

The very next morning after leaving the villa, John and I had a pleasant surprise as we cut into Highway 65 from the road from Barbarino towards Rinaldo's home in La Rocca.

The air was filled with the sweet familiar scent of freshly-cooked pancakes. There was a vanilla scent to these pancakes that many years after the war, I have never known anything else that would equal it.

It was six-thirty in the morning and that beautiful, sweet aroma hung low in the early morning humidity. On the left side of the road, we saw, for the first time, a roadside field kitchen had been set up.

I couldn't believe my eyes.

This kitchen had been set up to serve truck convoys hauling supplies up the Apennines. The idea to set up a mobile field kitchen for these hungry troops was really super and as John and I savored our breakfast of ham, eggs and pancakes, we asked one another, what else could we possibly have to make our life more enjoyable?

We felt blessed that things had always seemed to come our way.

1 told John in our whole time together, through all the risks we faced, we had been pretty lucky and at that moment, certainly knew a good thing when we saw it.

We hoped our luck would last as long as our desire was to enjoy it.

Surprisingly, it had.

When we rounded the big s-turn into the village of La Rocca, we noticed a crowd around the little shoulder of the road where we usually parked our jeep.

I felt something grab any insides and I looked at John. I could see he suddenly lost the fresh color in his cheeks.

When we pulled up, we could see a huge, black, burnt hole in the snow just off the shoulder right in front of Rinaldo's house.

We heard someone say that the Krauts had pulled in a railroad gun of their own on the other side of Bologna and began firing it towards La Rocca the night before.

A massive, railroad gun, just like I had predicted.

The shell must have been at least 350mm and weighed a ton.

The blast had blown molten metal shrapnel in every direction and left pock marks and holes in the walls of the surrounding buildings.

I didn't have the courage to look up but when I did, all I could see was a big hole in the room where John and I had slept.

The immediate sight was sickening; like looking at something dead.

My premonitions came back to me.

There was something that was going to happen to us.

1 couldn't say anything. I looked at John. Tears were forming in his eyes. All I could think was what we had said earlier: "We have always been pretty lucky." Slowly, we turned to one another, still visibly shaken, and went back down the stairs.

I had not yet noticed Rinaldo's wife and young son when John and I headed upstairs, but when we came down, I could see her huddled with her son by their stove.

She was still frightened, wondering what might happen next.

We walked outside their home and found ourselves looking squarely into Major Rigby's stern face. Lt. Frank Morang stood directly behind him.

I knew there was no use trying to wiggle out of the situation. The evidence against us was too convincing.

"Now where in hell have you two been?"

I don't know where I got the words from, but I said the first thoughts that hit my mouth.

"Major, it should be a comfort to you that we were not up there in that room as we should have been."

It was a long shot, but I needed something to take the immediate weight off of us.

"As to where we were, sir, I spent the night with a girl I happen to be in love with, near Florence. John went with me."

Now it was Morang's turn.

"You know, O'Connell, you were in an area off-limits. Know what you can get for something like that?"

I didn't care what the punishment might be. We were lucky to be alive.

John said, "Look sir, we've got our lives. That's a lot, believe me."

Rigby looked up at us. It was like he was looking at his kids who played hooky from school, but who knocked in the winning home run in an important baseball game.

"I guess we're all thankful that you weren't there early this morning." He started to leave, gesturing to Morang to join him.

"Come on, Frank."

Oh, by the way, stop by and I'll sign you each a complete clothing allowance."

After the two officers left, John took me by the shoulder.

"Boy, that's cutting it pretty damn close, Burke."

"Hey, where the hell's Snuffy?"

Just then, John and I spotted our driver, Snuffy Owens, lurking around the side of the adjoining house, keeping out of sight.

"Snuffy, just where in the hell were you when the Krauts fired their piece?"

We laughed as we heard him answer us in a sheepish low voice.

"Hell sarge, I was in bed having a good time with the Signora."

I couldn't help but laugh.

I don't know why, but what Snuffy said was the funniest thing I had heard or maybe it was the tension I had to let go of.

The improbable sight of this long, thin country boy from the mountains back home happily in bed with the dark, sultry Sardinian woman, just didn't set right.

Right or wrong, his evening of pleasure saved his life.

It didn't take Rinaldi long to get his family home patched up. He had enlisted the help of a mason in La Rocca who did all the necessary plastering work and a carpenter who helped him make a new window for our repaired room.

John and I contributed to the repair expenses which was not too much since most of the work was done for Rinaldi out of friendship.

The weather that week in November was warm and dry and plaster set fast and before long we found it difficult to see any remaining trace of the recent shell damage.

Chapter 9

Digging in—Fall 1944

Highway 65 was a tortuous, twisting and turning road through the highest pass of the mountains, the Futa. It was a fifty mile stretch from Florence, a long distance on that kind of road to drag everything we needed from gas, ammo, and down to Coca-Cola.

It had been originally built by the Romans and had not been bettered very much since. It was full of blind curves and steep slopes on the sides. It was hard to distinguish where the hard top stopped and the shoulders began; the mud and slush so covered everything.

In the back of my mind was the ever-present thought of the love I felt for Tina and the promise I made to her that I would come back to her when I could.

The sight of this one narrow, crowded, mud-covered road to and from the front lines made me believe that returning to the villa was impossible.

The torrential rains of October 1944 broke through the skies bringing with it the enemy's best ally, endless seas of mud and misery. If General Mark Clark ever entertained any ideas of spending Thanksgiving in the liberated city of Bologna, his silent enemy mud would forever change his thinking.

When John and I took our first look around Highway 65 when we arrived in the area, we both agreed as to what a hard winter our troops would soon face.

It was only mid-October, and already our commander, General Mark Clark had given the formal order that we would be digging in for the winter. There would be no attempt by our forces to advance any further north. We would face another long, cold winter of sweating out enemy artillery and mortar barrages and taking our chances on patrol duty.

It became a common opinion voiced by many American GIs who served there that the entire Italian Campaign was a brutal, but necessary holding action. The goal of the campaign was not so much to drive the German army led by Field Marshal Albert Kesselring out of Italy, but to engage some of Hitler's best trained divisions and keep them off the Western Front.

While this line of thinking made good sense on the Allied high command's strategic planning, it was a giant pain in the ass to the average American infantryman who would have to live it out in a foxhole on the side of a rocky, Italian mountain.

The Apennine Mountains stretch across Italy from east to west, dividing the country into two parts. There are rugged, steep, tortuous roads leading up from Florence through about five passes that range in height from six thousand feet. There are peaks jutting up above these ranges another two or three thousand feet. These peaks and high ground formed Kesselring's Gothic Line. Spires like cathedrals looked down on our every move. Behind these peaks spread well-placed German artillery.

The Germans had done a systematic job of pulling back into their Gothic Line defenses constructed by their slave labor units. What Kesselring had actually prepared was a hard winter for us. The U.S. Fifth Army had only one road north, Highway 65, over which to bring all our supplies to the front.

The strategy and planning of the high commands, the amount of work that went into the operations, the cost of the planes and bombs, and the destruction that followed all would have been in vain if they didn't eventually get a message from Charlie company saying, "Charlie company reports, mission successful, we have secured the railroad station and the market place; over."

No matter how much brainwork and planning goes into a combat operation, or how many tons of artillery shells must be fired or how many bombs must be dropped, you can never win without liberating the land actually held by the enemy.

Until one weary GI can actually stand in a village square, and raise his M-1 in the air and shout, "This town is ours," you haven't got a victory either.

John and I stopped by Fifth Army field headquarters on our way north from the Villa Calamai. We noticed their area had been considerably spruced up to include gravel walkways, a certain amount of planking on floors and almost everything neatly identified with proper uniform signs, each with the U.S. Fifth Army insignia.

We found the Army Pictorial Service tent with photo officer Major Linden R. Rigby inside and introduced ourselves.

Rigby was a product of the Hollywood studio system before the war. The two of us had always been so far away from headquarters that our handwriting on our film was better known than either of our faces. Rigby was a good-natured fellow, a bit older than either John or I. I sensed Rigby was really quite harmless in comparison to other Army officers I encountered who tended to bite at the slightest provocation, but thankfully Rigby, in our opinion, wasn't one of those.

Rigby had told us that we would have to check in while at headquarters with the II Corps Photo Officer, a position which had only recently been established and was now filled by Lt. Frank Morang.

Frank was different from Major Rigby in that he could bite without too much cause. Frank received a field commission for his meritorious conduct in the French Moroccan, Tunisian and Sicilian Campaigns. He was also a veteran of 25 years in the Hollywood movie business before the war.

He tended to have a slick way of concealing his real intentions behind his silver hair and sixty odd years. I had known Frank since we served together in Tunisia, and I had never been able to really figure the guy out.

But then, I was not alone in that assessment.

Frank certainly was cunning, sharp and gutsy on the inside yet on the outside, he seemed like some Ozark farmer. He justly earned the nickname that John and I affectionately gave him, "The Silver Fox."

In Tunisia, I heard that Morang often embarrassed much younger, 25-year-old lieutenants by giving them a hard click of the heels, and a snappy salute followed by, "Sgt. Morang, sir."

It got so embarrassing that some senior officer, who felt that maybe the man was too damn old to be just a sergeant, and he really carried himself more like a colonel deserved a proper battlefield commission. So I guess Morang's saying to us, "two wars and three revolutions," before at last being commissioned an Army officer finally did pay off.

The U.S. Army's II Corps was situated against a high hill that would protect it from incoming German artillery which was well within range.

Frank's tent was situated on the reverse slope of the hill. He had dug a large comfortable room out of the hill and then pitched his tent over it. He then lined the outer edges of his tent with large rocks. His home had become a well-constructed mountain refuge for a real mountain recluse.

Frank was a lone wolf. He was a wildlife type who took on a part of the rustic scenery that surrounded him. So much so, that he had trenched a gully that ran through his hut so that in the night after he had filled his bladder with all the wine he thought it would hold, he could just lean over and piss down the stream.

John and I wrapped up our visit with the Silver Fox during which we drank some of the lousy English tea, probably left over from Lt. Morang's North Africa days, and refused his offer to pitch a tent near his, telling him that we were city boys at heart and the wildlife of the mountains did not appeal to us.

We said our goodbyes, acknowledged that we were delighted to be under his protective wing and then excused ourselves.

Our driver, Snuffy Owens was once again swearing and bitching and trying to keep our jeep from being stuck. We were being slowed down by the heavy trucks in front of us that were getting stuck every hundred yards and looked for a way to get ahead of the traffic jam.

The road from headquarters led down towards a cow path which dropped off Highway 65 into to an area held by the "Blue Devils" of the Army's 88th Infantry Division. The 88th had recently gone over to the defensive and patrolled its improved positions and rehabilitated its combat troops as best as it could.

Snuffy eventually found a useful piece of hard-looking ground ahead of us and swung the jeep out from the road into a farmer's field where he thought he could pass the truck convoy. The field was muddy, but at least we didn't have anyone in the front.

Some MPs shouted to us, "Hey, don't you know those fields haven't been swept? There might be mines."

Snuffy didn't even look back at them when he shouted, "Sure, but if they mined the fields, they sure as hell mined the road."

Two military policemen assured Owens that the road in front of us had been swept.

But Snuffy told them that they didn't do a very good job because it was muddy as hell, and kept on going.

Pian Caldoli was a typical mountain village, made up of grey stone houses around a cobblestone square. It was so much different from the earth-colored villages of Tuscany. We found a woman washing clothes in a stream and asked as best as we could if she had room in her house for us. She apparently had done likewise for the Germans as she got the idea right away. The room she showed us into what must have been at one time a storage room. It was full of baskets, crates made of a type of cane and glass demijohns of wine. From the ceiling hung low strings of braided garlic, onions and red peppers, the kind that sell for $5 a string now. The walls were damp and small drops of water formed here and there. We wondered how that would be when it really got cold. We set up our cots, took off our boots and stretched out and passed around a bottle of Sarti cognac.

John took a drink and then said, "Well, this ain't exactly Martell. But then, this ain't exactly the Villa Calamai."

It was the first time we had mentioned the place. I guess each of us, for his own reasons, didn't really feel like talking about it, until now.

Snuffy poured himself a drink and passed the bottle to me. "You know, I'm gonna really miss that villa. All the people, they're really nice. I have never seen anything like that before."

"Not many like that in South Carolina, eh, Snuff?" John asked.

"Oh, they got some old plantations, but the villa was different."

Snuffy rolled over and looked at us. "You know, why in hell don't we just go back sometime?"

I raised myself up and looked at John.

"Might not be a bad idea, what do you say, John?"

He looked at me knowingly.

"I guess we could someday. We could go when the Lt. Frank Morang is not looking. Sure, why not? We'll have to try it out someday for size. It's a long trip. But I think we can do it."

John looked at me and smiled. It was comforting to know he had the same thoughts. John was a good "partner in crime."

The next day, we went past the 88th Division Regimental S-3 and then proceeded up the narrow road which followed a little stream that led between high hills. The area resembled a gorge and immediately gave you an uneasy, enclosed feeling. John and I soon reached a point beyond which no military vehicles were allowed.

We left Snuffy behind and proceeded forward along a dirt path with our camera gear. We soon heard some incoming German artillery coming over our heads but landing much further out of range behind us.

We arrived at a modest field command post which was manned by a handful of soldiers including a captain giving orders to a radio operator seated by his side and a couple of couriers waiting for instructions.

The shooting war began here. This was where large, planned infantry operations get reduced to a very personal affair. While John and I were actively scanning their positions, two stretcher bearers came quickly down the hill.

I looked down at the soldier lying on the stretcher. The guy lying on it must have been about my age. He looked peaceful.

I asked the medic, "Is he dead?"

The guy nodded.

"Funny, he doesn't look it."

The medic was chewing tobacco as he replied, and spit on the ground.

"Sometimes they don't. It just depends if they get it right."

The captain had finished his conversation with one of his couriers. I saw him turn to the medic and ask, "Where's he from?"

"He's from Lieutenant Clayton's platoon, sir."

The Captain turned towards me and sighed.

"I hope those replacements get here soon," he said, almost to himself.

That was it. No name, not a person, but one more casualty. That was the poor guy's official exit from his infantry company and the war.

All this young G.I. got was a quiet final look from an busy officer in charge and a spit of tobacco from a weary medic who had seen too many just like him.

His body would likely be taken to the rear by jeep and turned over to a Graves Registration Unit, placed in a mattress cover, and then buried along the side of the road in a temporary grave before eventually being shipped home. That would be the end of a guy who at this moment did not even look dead. He was probably one of Delta Company's riflemen, hit by a German sniper.

It was hard sometimes to remain callous and hardcore in the face of such tragic events.

How many I had seen and would see. Inside, it always did something to me. I felt an increasing sense of loneliness, rather than sadness. I felt bad for this poor guy, now all alone in the world, dead on strange soil.

John and I carefully climbed up the hill from where this casualty had come, hoping secretly that the next time a battalion aid man came down with the stretcher, he would not be carrying either one of us on it.

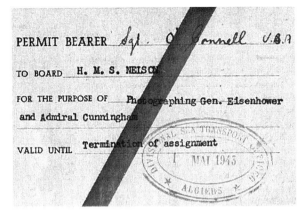

The assignment to photograph General Dwight D. Eisenhower and British Admiral Cunningham was one of Burke's first official assignments during the North African campaign and he kept his press identification card as a souvenir.

(O'Connell photo)

Still photographer Sgt. Burke O'Connell at left, walks parallel to General Dwight D. Eisenhower and British Admiral Cunningham during the inspection of British naval personnel onboard the battleship HMS Nelson in Algiers harbor.

U.S. Army photo

Secretary of War Henry L. Stimson greets General Dwight D. Eisenhower upon his arrival in North Africa. Stimson managed the drafting and training of 12 million soldiers and airmen, the purchase and transportation to battlefields of 30 percent of the nation's industrial output, and the building and decision to use the atomic bomb.

Army Signal Corps Photo, (O'Connell collection)

Army Chief of Staff George S. Marshall is seen in a casual setting seated with fellow officers at a briefing in North Africa.

(O'Connell collection)

Actress Martha Raye traveled extensively throughout the Second World War to entertain American troops overseas even though she had a lifelong fear of flying. Raye joined the USO soon after the U.S. entered the war and appeared with many of the leading comics of her day, including Bob Hope, Abbot and Costello and Jimmy Durante. Raye steps out, her suitcase in hand, from an Army jeep in North Africa.
(O'Connell Collection)

African-American soldiers enjoy an informal jazz jam session overseas. No official Signal Corps photo caption was recorded on the reverse side of this 8 x 10 original black and white print. In addition to their official duties, photographers of the Army Pictorial Service including O'Connell, frequently took candid still photos whenever possible at the request of soldiers they met to send home to family and friends.
(O'Connell collection)

Burke was often paired with photographer Earl Zeigler during his assignments in North Africa. Zeigler captures a relaxed British Prime Minister Winston S. Churchill as British Foreign Secretary Anthony Eden looks on.

Earl Zeigler photo, Army Pictorial Service.
(O'Connell collection)

General Dwight D. Eisenhower and Chief of Staff Gen. George C. Marshall confer.

(O'Connell collection)

French General Charles DeGaulle, North Africa
Photo by Burke O'Connell, 3131st Signal Service Company

French General Georges Catroux, Governor General of Algeria, 1943
Photo by Burke O'Connell, 3131st Signal Service Company

A feature story, published in an early February 1945 edition of Sunday Stars and Stripes Magazine, describes the challenging role of the Army Pictorial Service in recording the Italian campaign. Burke O'Connell is quoted in the last paragraph describing the difficulty of filming under fire.

Used with permission from the Stars and Stripes. © 1945, 2006 Stars and Stripes

This dramatic photo taken by photographer Sgt. John Mulcahy captures a German shell exploding at the instant of fragmentation in front of an Army truck in the town of Loiano. One man was wounded by fragments from the shell. The image became photo of the month by stateside U.S. photo editors and drew the attention of *Sunday Stars and Stripes* which featured the spectacular image in a feature story on Fifth Army photographers covering the Italian campaign. Highway 65 had been the main axis of advance during the October 1944 offensive. During a period of about five months, this road was under constant heavy German artillery fire.

Photo by John J. Mulcahy, 3131 Signal Service Company 111-SC-201289, National Archives

Army Pictorial Service photographer T/4 Daniel P. Phillips, 196th Signal Photo Company, takes ground terrain pictures. To get a complete view of enemy held territory, two or more combat photographers were often used.

Army Signal Corps Photo, 111-SC-380276

Florentines, returning to their homes after the liberation of the city, are seen picking their way across the Ponte Allegrezie, which spanned the Arno River until the bridge was destroyed by the retreating Germans. The people were willing to risk a ducking to get back, as shown by these catwalkers balanced on a rail of the blown-up bridge in mid August 1944.

Army Signal Corps Photo,
111-SC 192773-8

Historic medieval homes on both ends of the Ponte Vecchio were strategically destroyed by the retreating Germans, blocking any form of vehicular traffic across the bridge. Ponte Vecchio, Florence, Italy, May 1945. Photographers Burke O'Connell and John Mason drove what they thought to be the first Allied jeep across the Arno River bottom into central Florence during its liberation while assigned to a British Eighth Army scouting patrol.

(Photo by Donald Wiedenmayer)

Lavishly-painted interior walls and an open doorway into blue sky are all that remain of a bombed house at the end of Ponte Vecchio, Florence, Italy, May 1945
—*Photo by Donald Wiedenmayer*

Pedestrians and military personnel walk by the rubble of multi-story homes, many dating back centuries at the foot of Ponte Vecchio in Florence, May, 1945.
—*Photo by Donald Wiedenmayer*

Chapter 10

Thanksgiving, 1944

An Army maintenance section fills the roads in front of the villa, and electricity returns once more to the Villa Calamai as Burke, John, Tina and her family happily celebrate a traditional American-style Thanksgiving holiday meal, complete with turkey, pumpkin pie, and all the typical trimmings.

The oncoming winter weather grew colder and steadily crisper. The ground became hard and icy. Now and then, there were flurries of snow. Thanksgiving was only a few days away. John and I went to the ration dump to deliver some prints of photos we had taken of some African-American soldiers we met who were working at the supply dump. We intended to pick up some Thanksgiving special rations, which had been highly touted in issues of *Stars and Stripes*.

The ration boys were already in the Thanksgiving spirit, or I should say, spirits, for when we arrived they were singing and dancing around and having themselves quite a time. When I told them that we wanted to pick up a turkey, among other things, the head guy said, "Whatcha mean 'a turkey?'"

"You do mean *some* turkeys. Hey, Elmore, hit these photographers with some Toms."

The soldier standing in the chilled reefer and his helper soon started throwing turkeys out to us like they were going out of style. When John and I caught two, we began throwing the others back, as they kept being tossed back at us.

Finally, it was clear John and I wouldn't be leaving the ration dump without our quota of no less than five 25-lb. Tom turkeys.

The enlisted non-com in charge said, "How about hitting us with some more pictures? I got a lot of gals to send them to. I like that high, bright tone you get."

He was referring to the fact that the only paper we had was high contrast so naturally, all of the images of African-American soldiers we photographed emerged from the developer a little whiter in skin tone. In general, we didn't have an opportunity to use much color film in our official Signal Corps work while in Italy.

"Tell you what, Sergeant, we'll come back after the holidays and make some new shots. How's does that sound?" I asked.

"It jives, man; it really jives!"

Our little farm woman prepared one of the birds for us in her outside bread oven. We gave her one for her family that she made in a manner more becoming the Romagna kitchen. One turkey we had roasted and traded it off to a medic for six bottles of Four Roses. The other two turkeys were reserved to take to the Villa when we went on Thanksgiving Day, since John and I knew we would have that day off. The little shelf outside our window would keep anything frozen with its outside temperature of below zero. So at night, we would sit in front of the fireplace and eat turkey and drink Four Roses.

John would look at Snuffy and say, "Snuff, sure beats the hell out of South Carolina, now tell the truth."

"Hell, man, it's North, not South Carolina." Snuffy would take a drink and shake with the shivers. "You know, tell you the truth, we never had turkey for Thanksgiving. It was usually rabbit or some old wild goose."

I kicked his shoe with mine. "So, you see Snuffy, you've come up in the world. All the turkey you want and drinking Four Roses instead of that moonshine rotgut."

Johnny said, "Snuffy, maybe you should come back over here. Find yourself a nice farm girl like the ones around here and settle down."

"Are you kidding? Hell, they ain't even got a refrigerator or a washing machine."

"Have you got those down in North Carolina?" I asked.

"Hell no," Snuffy said. "But, by gosh, I could get them if I wanted them. That's if I had the money." He paused a bit and looked into the fire. "Hell, Burke, you're the one who should come back. That Miss Tina is a good-looking gal and she likes you, too. Yeah, you should come back."

I looked at him for a moment and then turned to John. He looked at me and then drained his glass. He wasn't going one way or the other. I took a drink and said, "You know, Snuffy, you might just be right." I lit a cigarette and thought as the smoke rolled up my nostrils. Yes, he could really be right at that, who knows?

Since Thanksgiving was going to be a holiday for us, we saw no reason why we shouldn't leave for the villa the night before. In that manner, John and I would have the night, the whole day and that night. Since no one could give us a good reason for not doing so, the three of us took off about four o'clock in the afternoon.

It began to snow that day and there was a cold wind. The skies were leaden and the temperature dropped. It was really getting to be like a Thanksgiving of old. With the barren countryside and the wind-swept snow, we missed only the one-horse open sleigh. Instead, we had an open jeep that rapidly filled up with snow as we went along. It was funny how fresh white snow hid the ugliness of the war.

The Allied tanks, guns, and stacked ammo formed a different pattern with fluffy white drifts on top and the darkness below. Even the burnt out vehicles and the black, distorted countryside became smooth and velvety under the fine sifted snow.

As we neared the downhill grade that led to Barbarino, it was dark, and the falling snow made such reflections that is was difficult to tell where the road ended and the slopes began.

The road was a designated blackout area and turning on the lights of the jeep was out of the question.

The weather got so bad in front of us that John and Snuffy got out of the jeep and held their flashlights close to the ground and guided me on the road. There were no guard rails or anything protective along either side of the highway.

Sometimes, John would slip into snow up to his waist and then yell at me to bear left. If we slipped off the road, it was at least five-hundred yards—straight down a cliff.

Gradually, as we descended toward Barbarino and we could see their lights as the situation got better and we could turn on our dim lights. Little by little, the snow lessened and when we got to the village, the snow was nothing more than sweeping flurries of dry whiteness that scurried along the barren countryside.

When we arrived at the villa's gate, a guard presented himself and asked not only who we were, but what we wanted there. We replied appropriately and finally he hoisted in his gun and told us what it was all about.

An Army trucking company of the local Transportation Corps had set up a maintenance section all along the village, street and into the farmyards of Tina's villa in Colli Alti.

Some of them had requisitioned another villa at the other end of the village for their use. There were ordnance maintenance trucks all over the area of the villa near the outside front gate. Some of the mechanics were living in the villa's separate farmhouse. Apparently, our requisition on the door signed by Colonel Vosbergh still held good.

The maintenance sergeant came out to introduce himself and soon everything was explained to the satisfaction of all. He knew all about us from Tina and apparently the villa was not to be touched. While we talked, the weather got progressively more overcast, and then all of a sudden, a roar broke out that sounded like a platoon of tanks taking off.

John jumped up and stammered, "What the hell's that?"

The Sergeant casually said it was their big generator starting up.

"You have a generator?" I asked. "It must be a hell of a big one to make that kind of noise."

The Sergeant naively responded, "It is. It could probably light up that whole village."

John caught my eye and we were both on the same track. "Well hell, Sergeant, if you've got that kind of current left over, why not pipe a line into the villa?"

The Sergeant didn't realize he had stepped too far. He looked thoughtfully at the villa not thirty yards away. "Well, I don't know."

I stepped closer to him. "Sergeant, just think of what it would mean to those people, after all this time, to have lights again."

John said, "Now look, if you need help, I used to be in a Signal Corps outfit . . ."

"No, I guess we can manage. I'll tell you. Don't say anything and I'll see what I can do."

Since the family never ate dinner until around eight-thirty, we were always there before. We unloaded all of the goodies in the kitchen. One of the turkeys I had agreed to make in the bread oven outside, just like the farm woman in Pian Caldoli. The other one they would eat later how they wanted. I told Tina that I wanted to make pumpkin pie and pumpkin just happened to be plentiful from all the overgrown squash in the fields.

We all went in to dinner, which was going to be rabbit fricassee, which didn't thrill John too much. But he made up for it by telling them of the impending surprise. It was always a Kaufman and Hart comedy to try to get something across. First, Rina, who always took the most difficult route to understand, and then the translation never got over too well with Signore Raffaello, who not only used the old classic Tuscany dialect, but was also hard of hearing. Tina, although she spoke good English, was a little rusty in picking up our fast, modern American language.

We were in the middle of this linguistic mishmash when, all of a sudden, blink, the villa's lights went on.

Tina, Rina and Signore Raffaello sat dumbfounded as though waiting for an explosion. The door from the kitchen burst open and Lucia and Beppa rushed in, screaming, "Signora, le luce, le luce!"

Everyone started to sing songs that apparently had something to do with lights. It was the light . . . no more darkness . . . it was like the end of the war.

It reminded me of when our convoy coming to North Africa went first near Tangiers. After many months of blackouts, to see a city lit up like there was no war was an unbelievable sight. Everyone came out on deck and started shouting and singing. Funny, these people reacted the same way that night.

The lights were not strong because the bulbs were for 180 V and the current we were sending in was only 110 V. But it was light and that's what was important. Tina ran through the house turning on every light she could find. I joined in. Signore Raffaello just sat there at the head of the table, his red face beaming, clapping his hands for every new light that went on. I can't imagine what Thomas Edison felt the night he lit New York, but I can assure him that the happiness and excitement ran through those electric lines certainly rivaled his feelings closely.

Later, the four of us sat around the fireplace enjoying a bottle of Four Roses, trying to do our best to conserve electrical energy, letting the dancing flames light our faces and make strange ballets across the wall in back of us.

"There has been much snow today in the mountains?" Tina asked.

"There's been as much as anyone could ask for. There are drifts there ten feet high."

"But you don't have to worry. The snow comes and goes quickly there. That's why Abetone is the only place near here to ski."

I said to her, "Hey, you sound like a real skier. Are you?"

"I was an intermediate champion," she said proudly. "Would you believe I came down the most difficult slope at Cervinia? It was so steep; you had to put on a special cape, like wings, so you could control the speed." She gazed into the fire. "Oh, how I love skiing! Do you ski?"

I nodded negatively.

"You'll have to try. It's a great experience."

"Did you ever fall, break a leg?"

"No, but once I broke a ski on a high slope and had to wait for the instructor to come up and get me. Then I had to come down on his back."

"I'll bet he loved that." I offered her a cigarette and lit one for myself. As I was doing so, I could see something was amusing her very much. "What is it? What are you smiling about?"

"Your hair; where do you get it cut?"

"Where do I get it cut? That's funny. Every two weeks, Army General Clark gives me a plane ride to Paris and we both go to Charles of the Ritz. Where do I get my hair cut? Hey John, did you hear that? Tina wants to know where I get my hair cut."

John walked over to us. "Well, I'll tell you, Tina. There's a chaplain's assistant near Monghidoro and when he's not helping the Chaplain with corpses, he cuts hair to pass the time away. So he cuts ours too."

"Hey John, you know I never thought about it until now. Do you think he practices on those stiffs?"

Tina threw her hands over her face. "I think you're terrible to talk like that!"

Rina came in with her late and brief English phrase, "What's stiff?"

Tina brushed my hair on the side of my face. "Anyway, you know what?"

I said I did not know what.

"I'm going to call you Gatto, because you look like a cat with the fur sticking out on the side of your head."

"Hey, I like that. I've never had a nickname in my life. I like that, Gatto, huh?"

"Alright, from now on, you are my Gatto."

"Don't people who have cats always pet them and kiss them and give them milk?"

"It depends on the cat and how good he is and, above all, where the cat is. If you are not a good cat, I will put you down with Beppa's cat."

"Oh God, please don't do that! Doesn't a cat have a first name? You know, like alley cat, crazy cat, or something else?"

She thought for a minute. "I know. I always think of you like a piece of blue sky in the darkness of the war. You will be a blue cat . . . yes, that's it. Gatto Bleu."

So with the name of the cat out of the way, we turned to dancing with old Bing going to "Amour."

The fireplace fire gently died down and the room got progressively darker and we danced closer and closer and the words of the song seemed to voice our sentiments . . . "seems I adore you . . ." The song seemed to trail off to distant places like the fire that grew dimmer and dimmer.

I held Tina close to me, trying to stop time, right there in that room. I knew that sometime soon our time together would run out, but while we could, we both clung to one another and that moment for all we had.

The very next morning, I busied myself in the kitchen preparing our Thanksgiving turkey.

Beppa was lending a helping hand furnishing all the ingredients needed for the stuffing. The stale country bread was ideal, but what really made the kitchen smell delightful were the big leaves of fresh sage being prepared, something I had never seen around my pre-war New York home.

While preparation of the turkey grew progressively more complex, all Beppa could be heard to say was, "Mamma Mia, che tacchino," which I took that to understand that ours was an amazing bird.

We finally put it in the outside oven where the bread was baked. The farmer's wife had heated it by burning large fascines of straw. We put the turkey inside and sealed up the stone piece on the opening with a mud paste to keep the heat in.

John, Rina and Tina had gone down in the meadow to find some dried leaves and branches to make some decorations for the table. Beppa had cooked the squash, so I seasoned it and made the pie. I mixed the dough in a large green ceramic bowl which I thought was ideal for dough since the others were metal or not large enough. I made the two pies and had them ready so when the turkey was taken out, they would be put in the oven.

When you have lived alone for many years, Thanksgiving doesn't mean too much. Most of the girls I ran around with in New York didn't have places large enough to house the kind of kitchen equipment that a Thanksgiving dinner calls for. Holidays, like Thanksgiving, are really family-type holidays that are shared by a group of loved ones. Without that, it gets to be just another special dinner in a restaurant. My first Thanksgiving in the Army was spent in North Africa only nine months after I entered the Army. The next one was in the mountains above Cassino where, if someone didn't mention it, it would have passed by unnoticed. This was my third one in the Army and the only one I have really remembered through the years. Rightly so, because I was with my best friend and the house that hosted us was warm and welcoming, as were the people in it. I was with a girl with whom I was falling in love, just how deeply, I would not let myself realize.

Rina and Tina very artistically decorated not only the table, but the whole room. They made motifs with pine cones, flaming leaves and shocks of green pine needles that formed a border around the villa. I leaned over to compliment Tina on the decorations, especially the colored leaves.

She looked at me, somewhat sad, and said, "They're turning to flame, like the song says. November's passing."

"But it also says that these moments I will spend with you."

At the end of the dinner, when Lucia came to pass around the pumpkin pie, which really looked great, she paused to whisper something to Tina. She broke out in a suppressed laugh. Her father immediately wanted to know the joke. She told him something in Italian which I was sure was not what Lucia had said.

She leaned across the table and said, "You made the pie in the bowl that our dog, Giovacchino, eats from."

That broke John up. "Oh boy! Well, Tina... look at it this way. Old Giovo is a great friend and anything that's good enough for him, has got to be good enough for us."

Rina, of course, came in late. "Giovacchino has eating the pie?"

To show that I was not in the least bit affected by the mixing bowl that belonged to the faithful setter, I took a big piece of the pie and proceeded to eat it. The pie was very good, even if I did say so myself. I said to Tina, "I should have been using Giovo's bowl all along, it's terrific! Try it or you'll hurt his feelings."

Finally, everyone was eating it and liking it. Maybe it was the bottle of Signore Raffaello's rare dessert wine, but the taste was really good. Since I felt he had deserved a piece, I took Giovacchino into the kitchen and gave him a piece of pie in his ceramic bowl. He probably liked it better there.

Chapter 11

Life along the front lines

By late November 1944, unusually heavy fall rains drenched Highway 65, pouring torrents of water down rocky mountain sides to gully dirt roads. Secondary routes were transformed into axle-deep sloughs. Dense, late afternoon fog regularly sifted down from Futa Pass, making Allied convoy drivers curse. Steady streams of heavy Allied military vehicles moved north to the front on battered Italian highways originally planned for pleasure cars and an occasional light truck. Side roads where ox carts once jogged were pressed into service by an army on the move.

John and I received new orders from Fifth Army Headquarters shortly after Thanksgiving to move further north from our present position closer to the front. I sensed our new move forward really was for the best.

We were assigned to cover a wide range of individual combat infantry units including regiments of the 34th Infantry Division, the 135th and the 168th. Our fellow photographers of the 3131st Signal Photo Company also photographed infantrymen of the 337th Regiment of the 85th Infantry Division.

Much of our specific work focused on the critical work being done by combat engineers of the 109th Engineer Combat Battalion who faced the thankless task of keeping the mountain roads leading north to the Po Valley open so that essential ammunition, food, clothing, replacements, and evacuation of our wounded from the front, could still get through.

The first snowfall of the season covered the higher mountains on November 11, 1944 and four days later two inches of snow and rain deluged the Apennines, and the real winter had arrived. The use of chains on vehicles, constant work by snowplows, and the almost never-ending hand labor by thousands of soldiers and civilians kept the roads open.

Up Highway 65 came a steady stream of equipment, food and clothing moved forward over Futa Pass and into the hands of combat troops holding the winter defensive line.

Our former living quarters that November had been in a damp, abandoned stone farmhouse in the tiny mountain town of Pian Caldoli, which was situated alongside a deeply rutted, nearly impassible muddy road which made daily travel to and from the front lines north of us always an improbability.

John and I drove our jeep into the outskirts of the ruined village of Loiano that forces of the Fifth Army troops now held and found two available rooms in the rear of a farmhouse which was protected by the slight slope of a little hill. We were still vulnerable to incoming salvos of German artillery which for now landed further behind us. We felt relatively safe, given our new circumstances.

The two rooms of the farmhouse offered us sufficient shelter. One room which we used for sleeping contained a large, working, stone fireplace, and the second, which we set up as a kitchen, featured an open pit, charcoal cooking grill.

John and I salvaged an Army field radio from the interior of a wrecked half-track and the ever ingenious Mason found just enough wire to extend out the farmhouse window to connect it to the working battery of our trusty jeep.

So, in the cold early winter evenings by the fireside, through a measure of hum and static, could each hear the British BBC confidently telling us that "their own Tommies were making important gains around Arezzo!"

Winter soon trapped the entire Fifth Army deep in the Apennines and short of the Po Valley. Day-to-day life along the front lines was for us was not very spectacular. We discovered there were really only two ways we could travel.

One was down the side of the hill at Loiano or the other was across an open stretch of Highway 65 that was fully exposed to the accurate, deadly fire of entrenched German heavy machine guns. Smoke pots kept along that open stretch of road did little to mask our travel, since strong winds kept the area fairly clear. Either way, you had the Germans looking down your noses. But I sensed they were generally interested in only our force's heavy convoy movements, so John and I traveling alone in our jeep didn't encounter anything rough.

Our day to-day still and motion picture coverage through the month of December seemed to get duller and duller as each winter day passed. John and I broke our tails just trying to find newsworthy subjects. During the day, damn near everyone, Allied and German, kept under safe cover.

At night, the never-ending process of patrol duty meant wandering off into outlying German outposts trying to get the drop on a couple of unsuspecting sleeping Krauts, and bringing them in.

What our brass ever expected to find out from these green German kids, I could never figure out.

I heard one tired American soldier, fresh from patrol, actually say to another, "Can you imagine that interrogator? He's asking him what he had for dinner."

John and I enjoyed a welcome break in the uneasy monotony of war when we went out to cover the arrival of a 240mm howitzer battalion.

The transport of such a massive weapon was not easy, and putting it in firing position we learned could take up to eight hours. The massive howitzer was the largest field piece used both by the U.S. and British armies in Italy during World War II and would look spectacular, captured on film against the beautiful backdrop of freshly fallen Italian snow.

Its 240mm shell weighed 360 pounds, and the piece required over a dozen men to operate it. Four men were required to load one shell which sent on its way, could strike enemy target up to 25,000 yards away.

We never did get the photographs we came after.

One of our tracked prime movers that was holding the howitzer back as another one gingerly pulled it down the hill into position suddenly broke free of its cable, leaving the massive wheeled gun free to take off thunderously at high speed down the hill, ramming anything in its path with its long barrel.

Fortunately, the men of this howitzer unit suffered no casualties, other than the immediate embarrassment of seeing this thirty-odd foot-long instrument of war lying uselessly on its side, as though gasping for its final breath.

If the Germans were watching from nearby Mount Adone, and I suspect they probably were, they said thanks for one Allied artillery piece which for now would not point their way.

The need for constant, healthy, combat-ready replacements plagued infantry companies on the front lines. The idea of designated replacement depots, referred to by GIs as "repple depples," was a logically sound one. Unattached, recently arrived soldiers shipped in from the U.S. were sent to a depot to await assignment. These new men had all sorts of military occupational specialties (MOS) that ranged from cooks, mechanics, musicians, clerks, to say nothing of drivers and painters.

Once they hit an overseas replacement station, they typically ended up assigned to the combat infantry units.

These Army troop replacement depots were notorious for grabbing any loose GI recovering from wounds or in transit they could find and then slapping him into the nearest compound destined for the front lines.

The reason for their lustfulness for flesh was that the Army never had sufficient manpower to satisfactorily fill their manpower quotas.

With the opening of the front in southern France in August, 1944, the Fifth Army was steadily drained of its reserve troops and replacements were hard to come by. During the winter of 1945, many cooks and clerks found themselves sighting down the barrel of an M-1 rifle instead of holding pots and pans and typewriters. But even these untrained, untried infantry replacements started getting scarcer by the day.

Any assigned GI who had been detached from his unit for a period of longer than a week was fair game and tended to be immediately assigned to a replacement depot for reassignment.

Such was my own case earlier in the Italian Campaign when I was released from a hospital in the Italian village of Avellino after recovering from an unexpected siege of malaria.

The two-and a half ton truck that took a load of us from the hospital I'd just been released from was headed for the "repple depple" on the outskirts of the city of Naples. When I saw the truck immediately take the turn toward Naples, in the opposite direction of the real front, another soldier and I seized our chance, and climbed over the rear tailgate and jumped out.

The whole incident passed unnoticed and within a day, each of us was safely back with our assigned outfits and certainly no one was ever the wiser.

It was during mid-December 1944 this time that something stirred the grey matter under Colonel Melvin Gillette's ever thinning hair. He came up with an idea which would have shocked even the blood-thirsty directors of Hollywood. The idea came down to John and I, and for what it was worth, was openly accepted by all available still and motion picture photographic teams of our battalion.

John and I would travel to a "repple depple" and pick out one poor bastard who was destined to go forward as an infantryman replacement. We would then follow him through his trip to join his new infantry company, observe him through his first combat duties, including his first, real taste of battle.

In other words, our assignment would be to follow him until (1) he was wounded; (2) or worse, he might be killed.

Somewhere along the line, I think Fifth Army photo officer, Major Rigby, decided to modify the story idea so that it was just a typical troop replacement story.

John and I went back one icy, cold morning to the Fifth Army Replacement Center, twenty miles back from our position with our driver Snuffy Owens.

The command was busily processing a large, fresh group of infantry replacements destined for the front then around Livergnano.

The two of us noted that it was hard to tell whether or not these young soldiers were shaking from the morning cold or from fear; maybe a combination of both. I knew from my own combat experience, that suddenly being moved up to God knows where and about to face God knows what, will make any combat soldier anxiously tremble with the best of them.

These new replacements were soon herded into 2-1/2-ton trucks, their gates pulled up and locked, and soon they were off to war. We followed their convoy in our jeep, making still photographs as we followed along. Somewhere near the front, Highway 65 had a straight stretch of road that had its left flank completely exposed to the enemy's potential fire power. The road then swung to the left between the relatively safety of two hills. There wasn't much you could do but drive fast and possibly say two or three equivalent Hail Mary's, hoping you could finish them.

We had traveled through most of the open road when it suddenly seemed that the entire German Army had opened fire on our little convoy.

Their machine guns ripped at the 2-1/2's, as they sent bullets bouncing all over the place. Thankfully, no one appeared to be hit. The Germans also mixed in some mortar fire for effect which landed just high off the road's shoulder and out of effective range.

John and I jumped quickly into a nearby ditch alongside the road. I yelled to our driver, Snuffy to leave, which he did with our jeep at full speed.

The new replacements were scattered all over the road, some flat in the truck and some behind the truck. From where we were in the ditch, we could shoot pictures without too much exposure.

A battle-seasoned sergeant jumped from a cab of the truck and yelled, "Get your asses back in those trucks and let's get the hell out of here!"

When the trucks started to move a little faster, some jumped in, and some ran alongside them. John and I took the chance and climbed over the little hill in back of the ditch, which immediately put us under cover. We picked up the convoy a little way up behind the hill.

We got to a point where no vehicles were allowed. The sergeant in charge ordered them all out of the trucks.

They were all looking at one another, beaming with the sheer joy of having survived under fire for the first time. Their sergeant let them each have their moment of ecstasy and then said, "Okay, you did real great.

You got to be foot soldiers fast. From now on, we will walk. That was the first but there will be more.

Just keep your eyes open and be ready to duck."

Their first sergeant now looked at them with a modest grin of satisfaction.

"Okay, you're now a part of Delta Company, so look sharp and alive.

Fall in, and let's get going."

As John and I walked off to below Livergnano, I felt that it's funny how fast any soldier can become a veteran. These guys already walked like real pros. As soon as they had three-day beards, you sensed you wouldn't even be able to tell them from the old heads.

These soldiers had acquired a fresh, proud, confident look about them. They were no longer dogs without tags in a 'Repple Depple.' Each was now an experienced combat infantryman, the very pride of the U.S. Army.

Now they each walked along as a proud part of Delta Company. Inside, I felt it was a shame they didn't belong to an infantry company with a name like Bravo.

Chapter 12

Merry Christmas, Gatto

Christmas, 1944

The gasoline pipeline story served John and I through the Christmas and New Year's holidays. Both Tina and Rina had made more decorations for our Christmas tree from pine cones and shocks of pine needles, and they did everything they possibly could to make the villa appear especially festive.

Since it was hunting season, the villa's kitchen was generally filled with freshly-killed pheasant and other wild birds that the farmer's son would hunt down in the meadow and in the surrounding hills.

Sometime before, Tina had told me of how a German infantry unit came to the villa late at night and took over all the beds and made her family sleep in the main dining room.

Their German occupiers stayed only a few days but long enough to make off with a significant amount of the villa's supply of sugar which they then had in abundance. In addition to satisfying their sweet tooth, the Germans also drank a considerable amount of the family's available champagne.

In order to chill the wine, the Krauts had cleverly attached individual strings to the neck of each of the champagne bottles and then lowered them into the well outside the villa where the water would chill them.

Tina had seen the Germans doing this and in order to deal them some mischief of her own, she cut some of the strings. At the same time, her faithful pet dog, Giovacchino, ate about a kilo of German butter and nearly died from it. All of these events brought Tina's whole family under very strong accusations from their German guests and they probably would have been dealt with in some severe measure had the unit not been urgently moved to the south.

My mind again wandered to the champagne Tina had spoken of, and I enlisted the aid of Ernesto and one of the farmers to see if we could recover some of those bottles lost down the well.

We fashioned a makeshift grappling hook and after several attempts, got nowhere fast.

Finally, rather than give up, one of the farmers disappeared and when he came back, he was wearing a pair of orange-colored rubber overalls and rubber boots.

It was obvious to each of us he intended to go down the well himself to retrieve the bottles.

We ran a sturdy rope through the pulley above the well and then with the aid of the farmer's son, we carefully lowered him down into the icy water. He got down in the well about chest high until his feet were on solid ground. He soon grappled around in the darkness and found one bottle.

Little by little, he retrieved eight ice-cold bottles of vintage Pommery Brut French champagne. There was no way I could get this helpful farmer to accept just one bottle for his important contribution to the effort. I later made it up to him with a generous amount of American pipe tobacco which he thoroughly enjoyed.

Tina and I celebrated New Year's Eve like I hadn't since I left New York City before the war. Soldiers of a nearby transportation unit came by the villa to join us, and one of them, named Frederico, entertained us with his accordion quite well.

Lucia, the family maid, invited some of her friends from the nearby village to join the celebration and soon nearly all of us were happily dancing throughout the villa.

Tina and I drank toast after toast. We found it almost incredible that we had known each other for five months since our first summer meeting in Florence.

In those past five months, Tina and I had managed to see each other with almost as much regularity as though we were just ordinary people dating in nearby cities.

We wondered how much longer our relationship could survive against the reality of war surrounding us.

The two of us walked outside the villa arm in arm to share a moment alone. The winter air felt calm, yet mysterious. Only from deep inside the villa did we still hear the sounds of celebration.

"Gatto, what will you do when the war is over?" Tina asked. "It has to end one day."

"You know, after you've been in this the way we have for a long time, you never really think about it. Funny, somehow you don't really care. You get to accept this as a way of life, just as though there are no tomorrows."

I drew her close to me.

"Since I've known you, Tina, I've begun to think about when it's all over. When I have a clear line of thought on it, I'll tell you. Right now, it's just an idea."

She looked deeply into my eyes.

"I want you to know I love you, Burke.

But that alone doesn't mean you are bound to anything. I know what I'm doing, just the same as you. I'm thankful for all the beautiful moments we've had together."

"As long as there is a possibility, you can rest assured I will come back to you Tina, however long it takes. I want you to honestly believe that."

"I do. You have already shown me that, my love."

I cupped Tina's face in my hands.

"Happy New Year, my darling. This is just the first. I know there will be more."

"I hope so. Happy New Year, Gatto."

Chapter 13

Reassignment

Spring, 1945

Throughout the winter months of 1944 and in the first months of 1945, German defenses were built up and reinforced in the city of Bologna.

On clear days in early spring, Fifth Army troops could see the buildings of Bologna and the towering peaks of the Alps in the background.

The weather began getting better and the snow was gradually disappearing. There was talk of a push as soon as the weather permitted it. One day Lt. Frank Morang came up to see us. We had an idea that he had plans to discuss since he had the look of a strategist.

"What I have to tell you, I want you to understand, has nothing to do with your not being here the night of the shelling. It's something that we have to do to create another team." John and I looked at each other, wondering what was coming next. "You two will be split up. We will add two other photographers and have a team more than we have now. What's coming up will need another team."

John and I both protested. We explained, as he well knew, that we worked well together and that meant a lot. But there was no way of convincing him since he washed his hands of the arrangement saying that it was Rigby who had been ordered to do so. So what he was saying was that an advance was coming up and we'll be leaving this area soon. He told John that he would pack up and go with Snuffy over to IV Corps which was in the westerly direction of Poretta Terme.

I was to be assigned a different still photographer, and another driver.

Just when John and I were happily congratulating one another with our luck, this had to happen.

I helped John pack his personal gear and camera equipment and load them into Snuffy's jeep and trailer.

We each tried not to be broken up by this but it was obvious that the unpleasant situation was getting to all three of us. We had been together as friends for a long time and while we took our association as a matter of routine life, we still had a close bond between us that I think few in our unit had.

I agreed with John that we would have to skip going to the villa for at least a week, so that I could see how my new partner would work out.

I didn't know who they were sending me and depending on whom it was, the possibility to return to the villa on a regular basis to see Tina might prove difficult, or worse, impossible.

It was still early in the afternoon when John and Snuffy left. I stood alongside the road, steps away from where the German shell hit, and waved them a reluctant goodbye.

I was all alone for what seemed to be the first time since arriving in Italy.

I felt the need for Tina even more than ever and I missed her immensely. I went back up to the little room where we had slept, which now seemed so much larger without the two cots belonging to John and Snuffy.

The patched holes on the wall seemed to watch me as so many eyes. I took a shot of grappa and sat in the corner on my cot. I realized that my loneliness was not my only preoccupation. I was beginning to feel a strong sense of fear for what might lie ahead.

Later, I dozed off and slept all night without taking off my clothes.

The next morning, I was sitting in the kitchen below having coffee when I heard the sound of a jeep drawing near.

I went outside and greeted my two new arrivals. The sight of a new jeep and trailer made one feel at least more mobile and somehow Tina now did not seem too far away.

Don Wiedenmayer was the photographer they sent to take Johnny's place. He was a tall, good-looking blond boy and the typical boy-next-door type. He had been with the outfit for some time.

Our new driver was Jim Morris. When I asked him if he had a nickname, he said Jim would be good enough. Jim was older than Don and I. He was not too tall and wore a thick dark mustache and long sideburns. I brought them into Rinaldo's kitchen and offered each of them coffee with a chaser shot of grappa. Jim smiled a bit and I could see that all of us would get along fine.

Preparations by the Fifth Army for its final spring offensive were visible everywhere.

Favorable spring weather grew better each day. The snow had all but disappeared except on the high peaks. The season was getting ripe for a push. A push meant moving away from Tina; this time for good.

All around there were preparations for mobility. Artillery was taken out of position and brought near the highway. Tanks and halftracks began to regroup. Near the front, in a large field, there was a sign designating it as a staging area. That was a jump-off point. The time was getting short. Late one afternoon, a young German lieutenant, who was the sole commander of their highest ground, Mt. Adone, surrendered. That was the beginning of the end. Without saying much of anything to Don and Jim, I took the jeep and said I would see them early the next morning. I couldn't do otherwise. It just might have been my last journey to Colli Alti and the villa and to Tina.

That night, Tina and I sat around the fire. It was a night of sadness no matter how much I tried to inject some ray of hope into it. There was no way of looking at it otherwise. This was our last night together. John had also seen the preparations in his sector. The next two days would see us on the move.

I told Tina that all we could do was to hope, but with the Po Valley ahead of us and then Austria and Germany, there was no telling where I would end up. This was the beginning of the final offensive campaign.

That night I gave her a buffalo nickel which I had carried for good luck ever since I enlisted in the Army.

"Here, Tina, I want you to have it. It's worked wonders for me so far."

She looked at me skeptically.

"Maybe if you keep it for me, this lucky nickel will help bring me back to you."

"I want to believe it."

Tina took the nickel in her palm and tightened her fist around it.

"I will believe it."

"I don't think that anything will ever keep us apart."

"It may take time, but I will be waiting for you."

"Somehow, somewhere, someone will help me and see to it that I will find you. Someone is protecting us, just like when that shell hit our room. Someone had a hand on our heads and protected us. We'll make it, somehow we will."

Tina was dry-eyed when I left her the following morning.

The morning air was crisp and cold, but Tina insisted on coming down to the massive front door of the villa to see me off. I quickly kissed her; she softly touched my weathered face and smiled. We were both feeling the same sadness. I watched her until I got to the outer gate, and then looking back, saw she was gone.

The trip up the mountain that morning was lonely and miserable. I had held back my tears when I left Tina, but now they came and I just couldn't hold them back anymore. I kept wiping my eyes with my wool Army gloves. What we had shared was real, and just couldn't now end.

The more I thought of Tina, the more certain I felt. Soon the tears dried up. Yes, the war would finally end, and damn it, heaven, hell or Hitler, I would make it back to Tina.

When I got to the village of La Rocca, Jim and fellow photographer, Don Wiedenmayer were standing in front of the house. The three of us each loaded our camera equipment and personal gear into the jeep and trailer and prepared to leave. Jim took the wheel and Don climbed in back.

Don immediately had a question. "Where do you think we are going today?"

Jim also looked at me as though he would like to know, too.

The events that led up to this point had me a little tight, and my response to the two of them was brisk.

"God damn, guys, where in hell do you think we're heading? Bologna!"

Chapter 14

Battle for Bologna

Burke O'Connell and his new partner, still photographer Donald Wiedenmayer film the intense battle for and the liberation of Bologna, the fourth largest city in Italy captured by the combined Allied armies on April 21, 1945. O'Connell is hopeful for a quick end to the war in Italy, but realizes that continued German resistance will require the pursuing Allied armies to drive farther from the Villa Calamai, closer to the Swiss border.

Bologna, Italy, Spring, 1945

To compensate for the unusually severe fall and winter weather, spring came exceptionally early.

In late March 1945, 15th Army Group finalized plans for its spring offensive and set April 10th when the British Eighth Army would jump off to clear the plain east of Bologna. The U.S. Fifth Army would join the attack on April 12, 1945.

Throughout the winter and early months of 1945, the Fifth Army prepared its physical equipment stockpiles for the upcoming attack.

Ordnance units were kept busy all winter rebuilding old and wrecked vehicles. Emphasis was placed on the rehabilitation and repair of all Fifth Army vehicles, weapons and field equipment, a task which was hampered by the low priority of the Mediterranean Theater in receiving new supplies from the United States.

Once the spring 1945 final Allied offensive began, there would be no stopping the pent up forces of the Fifth Army which was now under the command of General Lucian Truscott.

On April 20th, Allied troops drove north and poured into the city of Bologna from all directions. The fighting had been heavy on the outskirts, but with force on force to the Fifth Army's advantage, the German defensive line began to rapidly fall further back.

The people living in Bologna had endured a long Allied siege for nearly nine months, during which they felt the brunt of our artillery, bombs and strafing along their main streets. It was no wonder that their enthusiasm for us sent them yelling and screaming into the streets when we arrived.

Within the region, fingers of attack extended in many different directions. Our British allies had begun their push north advancing from the city of Rimini to Ravenna, the final resting place of Dante. Its operations area now straddled an area between the cities of Modena and Ferrara, squarely aiming at Verona.

The nationality of the troops streaming into the city was confusing to us so it must have been really confusing to the Italians. Italy had been the real melting pot of all countries who wanted to get their token bit into the fight so they could have a little say after it was over.

Fifth Army assigned the 91st Infantry Division, first largely African American combat division to the battle for Bologna, and they entered the city fighting alongside our Brazilian allies.

Mixed in with American combat infantry, there were the South Africans, then the English, then the New Zealanders along with their sphere of influence countries, then Poland and India.

We also had Jewish soldiers of the Palestine brigade enjoying, probably, their first real chance to get back at the Germans. Then to make the whole picture more confusing, there were the Italians partisans.

The partisans for the most part occupied themselves with shaving the heads of prostitutes and other females who were accused of fraternization with either the Germans or Fascists. The scene was brutal to the point of becoming savage as the women were herded through the streets accompanied by the jeers of the onlooking crowd. It was reminiscent of what the turbulent French Revolution must have been like on a larger scale.

The partisan movement in central and southern Italy was composed of a within-the-city force and once the city of Bologna was liberated, most returned to their normal lives.

The men were formed into brigades usually commanded by ex-military men and section chiefs from industrial work forces. They were skilled and highly trained, and for the most part, Communist.

The U.S. Army had done much to make the partisan movement effective in the north. They had trained men in the use of our weapons and explosive techniques and had dropped them behind German lines so that their combat knowledge could be put to good use. Allied pilots made frequent drops of ammunition, weapons, radio transmitting equipment and medical supplies of which only a modest portion ever found effective use against the Germans. I often wondered if we even supplied the paint with which they covered the village walls with "Yankee, go home" slogans.

Before evening darkness fell, Don and I returned to the village of La Rocca to pack our camera gear. The move had started and the village of La Rocca would become but one more memory in the distance behind us.

Jim left us with the jeep and drove back to nearby Fifth Army Headquarters to drop off our film for processing and to pick up more film. Don and I packed everything and arranged it in the trailer. Assunta made us some sandwiches from her country bread and salami, and Rinaldo made sure the three of us had enough wine to take with us on the journey ahead.

While Don and I waited for our driver, Jim to return, I walked across the street and gazed off into the sloping Italian hills which surrounded us. Only deep ruts crisscrossed in the earth where only a few days before, hundreds of soldiers and dozens of heavy military trucks, tanks and artillery had been.

I found it rather amazing how quickly large Army units can actually disperse when commanders issue an order to "go."

I guess that was what was in the back of my mind whenever I was with Tina. I knew there would be a "go" someday and that order from Fifth Army Headquarters would come to my unit fast, leaving only time for a short goodbye. I knew it had been always in her thoughts, too. We were both taking our life the way it was and when it was offered to us. But reason how I might, the sadness and loneliness still came over me like a fog, making it difficult to breathe.

The sun went down in back of the hills leaving La Rocca in a veil of purple. The emptiness of the fields with their zigzag patterns became scary to watch. It made me remember the sadness I felt when, as a boy, I passed the ground where only the night before the circus had glittered in full splendor. To see it empty seemed such a pity and I asked myself why it would not remain forever. I guess I was telling myself that I wanted the Army to remain where it was; not to go away. We could all stay there. But that was not possible and I knew it but it was pleasant to think about.

When Jim returned, we hitched up the jeep and trailer and began saying our good-byes to the people in La Rocca who had been so hospitable to us. You get to form a kind of bond with these people when you have stayed with them and have tried to understand their life and its good and bad features. There were tears in their eyes when we embraced for the last time.

As we drove away, Rinaldo and Assunta stood near the road and waved to us. As I looked back, it seemed that I could still see the fresh shell hole in the side of the house and the black burnt scar on the road where they now stood. I knew the image was just a vision of the past, and like all visions, gradually faded away in the distance.

Don and I arrived in the city limits of Bologna just before evening and hoped to quietly unload our camera gear. The nearby Germans threw out a welcome artillery barrage along Highway 65 just to greet us.

I guess the Germans guessed that it would be open season with all the Allied truck convoys moving up, but their aim was not too good. We bivouacked in a park where a 752nd Tank Battalion outfit had done the same thing. It is always comforting to have all that heavy iron around, should unwelcome enemy shells suddenly drop in on you.

The two of us made some quick coffee over our Coleman stove and ate some canned K rations for dinner. Our meal was a far cry from what I had become accustomed to while living at the villa, but then, I thought, every once in a while, you have to live like a soldier, and eat like one as the night sounds of incoming German artillery grew steadily nearer to our position.

A solo German Luftwaffe plane came buzzing by to find a lucky target to drop his bellyful of bombs on.

Don and I recognized we didn't stand much of a chance of sleeping well that evening so we dug out a few bottles of wine and decided to enjoy them.

After a night without sleep, Don and I were glad to be on the road the following morning with our jeep following the advance north.

We drove from Bologna in the general direction of Mantova by traveling a narrow gravel provincial road.

We noticed there were an abundance of small, dry streambeds in the area we traveled.

Since most of the bridges in the immediate area had been destroyed, Don, Jim and I tried to cross each stream as safely as we could.

We were soon ready to cross a deeper stream that carried a little more flowing water within its banks than usual.

Just to be on the safe side, Jim took the fan belt off our jeep in case the water got too deep. While we began to cross what looked like a dry portion of the river bed, a ragged group of Italians came up to our jeep begging for all sorts of things that didn't make too much sense to us.

We saw a young mother with a small swaddled baby. I began to get the idea that they wanted us to take her across.

I soon looked at Jim Morris and Don. Both shared the opinion we didn't face too much risk since the depth of the water appeared to be very low on the other side.

Our driver was certain the motor of our jeep would not get wet enough to stall.

I helped the young woman and baby into our jeep and once everyone was in place, we began our riverbed crossing. We didn't have any problems most of the way across, but just as we drew within yards of the shore on the other side, our jeep began to suddenly sink.

We had apparently found a section of the riverbed where the bottom dropped off. The engine started rumbling and our usually rugged jeep sputtered and stopped. Cold water soon began to flood our jeep until the seats were completely covered.

The young mother could not swim and began to panic, quickly jumping out with her baby into the water.

Don jumped out of our jeep to catch our still camera cases and Jim did his best to hold the jeep in place before the moderate current could sweep it down river.

I soon found myself in the water where I got a hold of the young woman and her child and carried them safely towards the nearby shore where others were now waiting to help us.

Fortunately for us, there was a weapons carrier nearby who tossed us a tow cable which Jim soon hooked up to the jeep's bumper and we were pulled out of the drink in no time.

The weapons carrier towed us until the jeep's ignition dried out and turned over. After that we found our road and took the direction for Mirandola, which was the way the traffic was headed. One just follows the advance because that's where the enemy is.

Late that afternoon, we ran into a fire fight during which some of the local oxen got caught in the crossfire. Local farmers ran out and tied ropes to the dying animals and dragged them off toward a nearby large agricultural compound.

Don and I had taken shelter behind large, brick structures which probably dated back to the fifteenth century.

Since it was getting late in the afternoon, we thought that we might as well stay here since they weren't hurting for room and from what we could gather, the people there wanted us to stay.

The compound must have housed five or six families. The men began hoisting up the killed animals and dressing them while they were still warm. The women, there must have been thirty, started rapid and mysterious preparations in the various rooms around large open fires. Some of the men came from the cellars below ground with baskets full of bottles. We were to find out later that the bottles were Lambrusco, a charged red wine, slightly sweet, famous in the Modenese area.

While pasta was being made, meat was roasting on the spit and bottles of Lambrusco were being opened. The stuff was highly carbonated and as each cork went flying off into the air, at least a half bottle went foaming up into the faces of the laughing people gathered around.

The scene reminded me of the Prohibition days when my brother James and I made home brew. It was really great, as many of our friends agreed—providing you can catch enough of it to drink. We managed to catch enough of the Lambrusco because little by little, everyone became Maria and Luigi which must have been the first two names we heard. We, of course, became known to the locals as simply Joe and Johnny.

The meal was finally spread out on a long table and we sat around on long benches. There was an endless array of meat dishes; after all, an ox can weigh in at 1,000 lbs., and there were two of them. Not that both of them were cooked but something had to be done with them because refrigeration was not around. The pasta dishes were numerous and plentiful.

Accordion music began to play and the louder it got, the more the Lambrusco seemed to flow.

Some of the infantrymen who had engaged in the fire fight earlier came in and if the war ever stopped for a few hours, it did that night. How we ever got to our cots, I'll never know.

I awakened the next morning not knowing where I was or how I even got there. My mouth felt like I had slept in it with my socks on. We made some coffee which was about all we could think of getting down. The place was surprisingly quiet.

While Don went down to the jeep for something, Jim said to me, "Burke, you're alright. You're a nice guy. I thought I'd tell you."

"You don't have to, Jim.

We're not together to make each other happy. But I'm glad you think so. The feeling is mutual. I liked the way you got us out of the river. You know what you are doing."

"So do you. I really admire the way you got that woman out. That was good."

"Don't be too hard on Don. He's okay. Now let's get out of here before the war runs out."

As we were going down the stairs, he said, "You know, I was a dice dealer at a joint on the West Side of Chicago."

"I hope no one rolls you some flats in this game we are in."

That day we took the main route, Highway 12, to Mirandola. The whole section was a network of small provincial roads that went in irregular directions. It because almost a comedy of errors as we ran into units asking which way was what town. Recon units were running into each other while going in opposite directions. Small, detached Kraut units were found standing along the dusty roads asking for a lift to somewhere, from one side or the other, it didn't make much difference.

We were stopped by two Germans waving a white flag. When we stopped, they said in good English that they wanted to surrender their whole unit. Their unit turned out to be a large contingent of about seventy-five men and twenty vehicles. It was apparently an administrative unit bivouacked beneath some trees. I told them just to hang on, throw down any weapons, hang out white flags and keep some lookouts on the road waving white flags like mad. I explained the risk they would run if a fast-moving tank unit came by and started firing the minute they saw Krauts.

While there were German units willing to surrender, there were others who pretended to want to surrender and then opened up at close range. Many of our recons were sucked into phony situations only to be blasted unsuspectedly.

Don and I passed little towns where depressed German paratroopers sat almost unnoticed on the curbstone, while the townspeople cheered onward our armor and men. It must have been a disheartening thing for these men. They had given what was asked of them; right or wrong, they had given. Now they were abandoned in a country which was not theirs and were not even given the dignity of an official surrender. They were left to sit alone while the war passed them by. They were expendable. They were a commodity that had outlived their usefulness. The Italian farmers, who only a few days before would have gladly shot them down, did not even bother to cast a resentful eye towards them.

We came upon two recon units who had just blocked in an intersection where a large personnel carrier was traveling, almost as though in the wrong direction. The two units hit the carrier with their 75's and the German vehicle, blasted open, spilled over on its side. We examined the unit with the recon men. There must have been maybe twenty Germans in it. Now they were blown to bits and scattered all over the area. Only the two in the front remained intact. One of them, obviously in charge of the food detail, was a young boy of about twenty. He was upside down in the front seat, his long blond hair hung down. The large thermal food container had overturned in his lap. His whole body was covered with spaghetti. The red sauce ran over his chest and down his arm to the ground where it formed a small pool. It was so incredibly grotesque that only Dali could have thought of it. But Dali wasn't there. This was real. I have never eaten spaghetti with tomato sauce since then, that for a fleeting moment I am not reminded of that scene somewhere on the back roads of Mantova.

The U.S. 88th Infantry Division began a rapid 20-mile march towards Verona by foot, jeep, captured German vehicles and even by bicycle, covering a distance of 40 miles in 16 hours. The fast-moving division reached the outskirts of Verona by daylight on April 26, 1945 and soon cleared the city from German resistance.

The Germans in their flight left all non-essential supplies and equipment behind in their retreat.

The fields were full of cattle and horses of all breeds, taken probably from the provinces below the valley. Civilian cars that had been "requisitioned" bore the license plates from far away Naples and Rome, and even as far south as Palermo and were jammed into the fields in among the cattle.

Heavy fighting continued in the outskirts of Verona. This was natural since it straddled the main east-west highway from Turin to Venice. Both directions offered the Germans escape possibilities. The local partisans were heavily engaged with both Germans and civilian-clothed Fascists. When our tanks moved in, the resistance lessened. These rear guard actions were necessary to let the German troops pull back to other lines of defense, but they were quickly being liquidated by the Partisans and GIs.

Inside the city of Verona there was an air of anxiety and nervousness. There was none of the cheering and flower throwing as had been the case in the cities to the south. Up to Verona, the advance had been a real rat race. It was unbelievable that an attack could turn out to be a marathon. It was like a maneuver. They were a sad bunch, the Krauts we picked up there. They were much different from the first I had ever encountered. That was in Tunisia. A German prisoner spit in the face of his interrogator and only the quick hand of a POW non-com who wanted to play it by the book, saved him from being blown to hell and back.

We were then receiving the first results of a full scaled retreat. Now they would slow up and ask for terms. I would be lucky if the war ended right then and there. It would not be too far to go back to Colli Alti and the villa. But the Germans were not giving up, at least not for a while.

Don and I met up with another team of photographers from the 196th Signal Photo Company headed by Sgt. Martin Brooks. Brooks was a few years' older than I was and had a sense of humor that made you think he took the entire war in stride. His claim to fame, if he ever would claim one, was that he was the brother of the popular American silent film actress, Louise Brooks.

Since all four us were going more or less in the same direction, we decided to join together and head toward the city of Treviso which was located between the Gulf of Venice and the Alps.

Donald Wiedenmayer,
Cocoa Beach, Florida, 1997

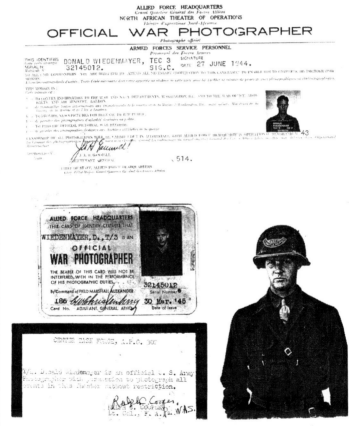

Special thanks to Donald Wiedenmayer for sharing copies of his own press credentials from his service in the North African and Italian campaigns. Allied Force Headquarters issued war photographer identification cards to O'Connell and Wiedenmayer on the same day, March 30, 1945.

—*Photo by Donald Wiedenmayer*

Two Catholic nuns enjoy an unexpected Allied uniformed military escort while on an outing in downtown Florence, Italy.
(O'Connell collection)

One wonders what became of this smiling, young Florentine boy in the years after the war in Italy.
(O'Connell collection)

A young Florentine girl accepts the welcome gift of chewing gum from an American serviceman. If Hershey's chocolate and Wrigley's chewing gum ever acknowledged their commercial success in Europe long after the war, much of the credit should be properly given to the average American G.I. who did one hell of a great job of free advertising as they handed out samples wherever they served all over the world.
(O'Connell collection)

An affectionate Burke O'Connell takes a playful moment to "embrace" ancient Roman history.

(O'Connell collection)

An armed and hilarious Burke O'Connell, left and John Mason, far right, mug for the camera. Fellow photographer, Marshall "Sonny" Diskin, holds a flashbulb.

(O'Connell collection)

Burke O'Connell, John Mason and their driver, Snuffy Owens.
(O'Connell collection)

O'Connell prepares to press the shutter of his wine bottle camera in this playful multiple exposure black and white print.

(O'Connell collection)

Burke and partner, John T. Mason wonder where they put their last bottle of potent Italian grappa.

(O'Connell collection)

Burke and John are all smiles as they enjoy a balcony view of Florence with a local family.

(O'Connell collection)

Burke walks through the Florence American Cemetery. 1944.
(Photo by John T. Mason, O'Connell collection)

One of my favorite casual portrait photographs of Burke revealing behind him a panoramic, almost postcard scenic view of Florence.
(Photo by John T. Mason, O'Connell collection)

Burke pauses to adjust his camera case while a well-dressed Florentine pauses to take notice. 1945.
(Photo by John T. Mason, O'Connell collection)

Burke looks sharp in his garrison hat, shirt and tie. Army photographers were required by their commanders to maintain proper uniform appearance while in the field.
(Photo by John T. Mason, O'Connell collection)

Swirls of ancient cobblestones, Italy.
(Photo by John T. Mason, O'Connell collection)

Allied troops march through the center of Florence, Italy.
(O'Connell collection)

Bomb damage opens the shattered interior of an unknown historic Italian church to the sky.
(O'Connell collection)

Shadows and light bathe the silhouette of a young Italian woman and young girl kneeling in prayer in the battered ruins of a Catholic church. The poignant photo was entered by O'Connell in a *Life Magazine* photo contest after the war.
(O'Connell collection)

Chapter 15

Sightseeing in scenic Venice

Venice, Italy, 1945

The theory behind still and motion picture coverage by the Army Pictorial Service in cases like these is to link the Army with important historical landmarks that people back home could relate to.

So on May 1, 1945, we made a personal "conquest" of the city of Venice with two gondolas and four sharp-eyed Army Pictorial Service photographers.

The British Eighth Army had smashed the German Tenth Army, taken the port city of Venice, on April 29, 1945, and were then driving rapidly towards Austria and Yugoslavia.

I kept for myself a print of a black and white Signal Corps photograph taken by Don Wiedenmayer in Venice showing my friends Martin Brooks and Sam Spirito in the second gondola enjoying the sights of the city which we submitted to the Fifth Army Photo Officer for their consideration.

Our weathered, olive-drab field uniforms didn't somehow match up well against the beauty of the Piazza San Marco, and soon we were the subject of curious gatherings of people. The local partisans were much too busy again taking their own suspicious citizens to the local Questura, an office of the Italian state police for questioning to pay us any mind.

We hadn't explored too much of the city of Venice when we encountered two young men whom, in spite of their clothing, clearly had all the appearance of being American written handsomely across their faces.

The pair attempted at first to dodge us, but we finally cornered them. We discovered the two young men were two Army Air Corps fighter pilots who had flown their missions from Peretola Airport near Florence before being shot-down by the German Luftwaffe two months before.

Friendly Italian partisans had picked up the two pilots and transported them to the city of Venice for safekeeping. The Germans had considered the historic city of Venice off-limits to all but their higher-ranking officers during their occupation, so it was comparatively safe for two Americans living life on the lam.

They had been furnished civilian clothes and had been living comfortably with a local Venetian family near San Marco Square. Don and I soon discovered each had acquired some pidgin Italian which came in quite handy when they ordered us drinks for themselves in the local square.

They reluctantly told us they were afraid that we might turn them in to the nearest military police and break up their fun. It was clear they had been having a ball and just wanted to stick it out in Venice for a while longer. We agreed that we wouldn't turn them in, and took them up on their invitation to a small Venetian restaurant they recommended where we were offered plenty of wine and treated to a fine lunch.

We gave each of them most of our cigarettes since that seemed the only personal necessity they had been sorely missing.

The two pilots had exchanged their American dollars for Italian and had received a handsome rate of exchange from Venetians who wanted to have a greenback in their pockets rather than a dubious lira.

Their Venetian hosts owned a small souvenir shop, so we did what every tourist tends to do while in Venice. Each of us purchased all sorts of trinkets, mostly in hand blown glass. All of it made me think of Tina as I had seen many things in Venetian glass in the villa. I wanted to be in Venice one day with her.

Maybe someday after the war we would travel there and do some sightseeing of our own.

I reached over and picked up a little black moor statuette in black, red and gold. I thought by buying the gift for Tina at that moment, I would have an opportunity to see her once again. Whatever my reason for doing so, the statuette would be a modest gift when, and if, I did see her again, it would tell her that I had been thinking about her even though we were far apart and our lives had become more confused than ever before.

Our two fighter pilot friends accompanied us back to the gondolas. They were two nice kids and were getting their shot at a real restful vacation after many combat missions without any official rest and relaxation leave.

Each of our gondolas lazily cut through the murky water. We saw very little water traffic from nearby motorboats and the going was smooth. Brooks and I mused to one another how strange a war can get.

To each of us, our visit to Venice seemed like a private guided tour and we enjoyed every moment of it as if it was our last chance to experience the rich beauty of the city. As events unfolded, our visit to Venice was exactly that—our one and only chance.

By late afternoon Don and I returned to the village of Treviso just in time to see thousands of fresh German prisoners being brought back down the road that in the other direction could once have taken them to safety in Germany, but would now lead them to an Allied prisoner of war compound.

The city streets of Treviso were soon filled with these dusty, disheartened German infantrymen, many of them mere boys, since their beloved Fuhrer, Adolf Hitler had been scraping the bottom of the barrel for some time.

Their disheartened faces showed expressions of utter futility and disbelief. You could sense even they wondered to themselves how such a proud, mighty army could have been reduced to a shuffling shamble. Don and I stood watching a lengthy column of Germans passing by in route step, and then looked up to my left to see a mud-splattered jeep draw near. The jeep had Canadian Army insignia on its front bumper, which wasn't at all unusual, since their infantry had been fighting the Germans in the same general operations area that we had been in. The jeep's front windshield had been thickly splattered with mud and was not at all well cleaned by its twin working wipers. Its opaque side curtains obscured my view of the driver and any other occupants inside.

I wondered why four Canadians might be going in this direction and why they wouldn't at least have sufficiently cleaned their windshield to see the road in front of them.

The jeep then stopped not more than five feet from me, since the street was by then filled to capacity with American soldiers. I had sufficient time to lean closer towards the jeep's side curtains and what I saw made me immediately pull my Army .45 from its holster and say to fellow photographer Sgt. Martin Brooks, who was then standing not far away from me to immediately come towards me.

Brooks covered me while I pointed the muzzle of my .45 at the driver, who appeared to be a high ranking German officer, and told him to quickly step out of the jeep if he valued his life. The other remaining occupants of the captured Canadian jeep were also German officers and they knew by then they had no other choice but to surrender. I watched as they glumly filed out from the jeep, hands high.

The two of us pulled off two Walther pistols, a Luger, a pair of field glasses, and a decent still camera from the Germans.

A passing American military policeman briskly walked up to one of the surrendering German officers and snapped off a large Iron Cross insignia from his neck before proudly walking off.

One of these two captured German officers politely asked me in halting English, where our troops would soon be taking him.

After all I'd seen since the war began, why I thought, shouldn't I have the personal satisfaction of a single German surrender of my own?

"Just do an about face, and follow the crowd. You're all going to the same place."

The dejected German officer was soon seen shuffling off in the same direction as the soldiers he had once commanded.

The next morning, Don and I drove our jeep over to the 91st Division field headquarters where we learned our superiors at the 196th Signal Photo Company headquarters further south in Caserta had an urgent message waiting for us.

I found it incredible within the chaos of war that the Army could still put a single finger on one single soldier with a single teletype message if they genuinely wanted to.

During the same time II Corps had pushed north towards Verona, IV Corps, which included the 10th Mountain Division, had by April 26, 1945 moved up the east shore of Lake Garda toward the exits of the Brenner Pass. The division faced some of the most difficult fighting it had ever experienced since the breakthrough towards the Apennines.

We received new orders signed by Captain Ned R. Morehouse, Fifth Army Photo Officer and dated May 2, 1945, to proceed with no assigned date to return, from our present location in Treviso, a distance of seventy-five miles west to Lake Garda where we would join a temporary photographic mission to help provide photographic coverage of the 10th Mountain Division leading us to one of the most unusual situations we ever found ourselves in during the entire war.

Chapter 16

A race to the Alps

Swiss border, 1945

It seemed at that time, the Germans were urgently trying to make a separate peace for the Italian front. Behind the scenes negotiations were busily going on at General Mark Clark's 15th Army Group headquarters in Florence.

At that time there was sort of a truce in effect between Allied forces and the Germans until the final written terms of the surrender agreement could be signed.

But at the same time, the Germans who remained were well armed and on alert. German commanders were afraid of the Italian partisan action against them in retaliation for some of the atrocities their personnel had committed.

General Clark did not want these retreating German troops to escape through the Brenner Pass into Austria, which was still under their control.

Soldiers of the 10th Mountain Division and 85th Division crossed the Po River and moved towards the Alps starting on April 23, 1945.

Clark ordered Lt. General Lucian Truscott to send his Fifth Army combat troops up the Brenner Pass as quickly as possible to close the border. The important task had been assigned to a combat team of infantry and tanks of the 10th Mountain Division.

Soldiers of the 10th Mountain moved up the east shore of Lake Garda toward the exits of the Brenner Pass and in the demolished tunnels of the east lake shore drive ran into the most difficult fighting they had had ever experienced since the breakthrough in the Apennines.

When Don and I arrived at the 10th Mountain field headquarters from Venice to report our arrival, I discovered my old friend from New York, Garnay Wilson, seated behind a field desk as if he were waiting for me to show up.

Garnay and I had once shared an apartment in New York City before the war, and while it appeared to my old friend the Second World War might pass him by, Wilson was finally drafted by the Army and eventually assigned to a tank battalion.

Clearly, Wilson wasn't what you would describe as any form of tank material, so he became the commanding officer's chief administrative aide and liaison non-com. I wasn't surprised to see him enjoying the comfort of a senior officer's personal chair doing his daily paperwork when I laid my eyes on him.

Wilson didn't seem at all surprised to see me.

"When our C.O. said we needed to have photographic coverage of this task force, I told him to get you, if he could.

He got a hold of Fifth Army, Photo Officer, Captain Morehouse just to find you."

The orders I received directed my photo team and driver to check in with 10th Mountain Division headquarters and report to 2nd Lt. Francis P. Mulhair who had been assigned to lead the detachment of 196th Signal Photo Company personnel assigned to the mission.

Garnay told me that the day before Don and I arrived at the shores of Lake Garda, Italian dictator Benito Mussolini had been picked up by partisans in nearby Dongo and there by the shores of Lake Como, was ordered shot. His mistress, Clara Petacci, died beside him.

Our 10th Mountain Division task force left Lake Garda in the late afternoon on April 30th, 1945. The force consisted of two tank platoons and one platoon of infantry, plus some special heavy weapons. We were slowed in our progress by light rains and dense, morning fog. I had the opportunity to ride with Wilson and the task force commander in his jeep which had radio coverage for all participating units.

The road march towards the Swiss border was gong to take 250 kilometers to complete over some of the worst roads in Italy.

Every so often we came upon a German road block. I watched as our task force commander and his German-speaking interpreter would get out of our jeep and explain what our mission was all about. The German sentries would then allow us to pass some high-ranking German brass which also happened to be traveling by vehicle in the same direction as we were. Occasionally, we would have to stop and explain the purpose of our mission all over again.

Sometimes our explanation worked the first time, and periodically we would come across some German sentries who had not yet received the word that German forces in Italy had officially surrendered and he would have to call up ahead and get the necessary authority to allow our vehicles to pass.

All of us shared the same uneasy feeling as we drove past all of those still-armed German sentries, and there were many, and looked down the barrels of all their anti-tank guns pointed directly at us, that this was one hell of a way to win a war.

At one point, late in the night, negotiations to allow the task force to move forward did break down and we had a long wait before a high-ranking German officer could get verbal clearance to move on.

Some of the tankers expressed the feeling of "to hell with the Krauts, let's just push on through." I thought of what could happen in our current situation if the tables suddenly were reversed and the Germans did not surrender to General Mark Clark down at 15th Army Group headquarters in Florence.

When I mentioned the tanker's thoughts to the captain directing the task force, he shared the very same concerns.

"I sure hope they know what they're talking about down there and don't get the words messed up. This could sure turn into a real mess."

It was in the early hours of the morning when our task force arrived in Bolzano at the two main roads which led to the Austrian border.

One road lead to the Brenner Pass and the other road lead through Merano to the Resia Pass. The task force split up and Don and I accompanied the part that went on to Merano towards the Resia Pass.

When Don and I drove through the Italian city of Merano, the area was still dark and deserted but Don and I arrived at the Austrian border just as the sun came up on a most beautiful rural scene. There were three Swiss border guards at the barrier and it was impossible to explain to them why we were there.

The sight of those American tanks blocking the road and the infantrymen all around the fence gradually gave them the idea. So they went back to their guardhouse where it was warmer. They were probably thinking that it was the problem of the Wehrmacht to fight the Americans, certainly not that of the Swiss Frontier Guards.

When General Eisenhower invaded North Africa, he described an arc that would become a circle. His famous Crusade in Europe described the other part of the circle. To make it a full 360 degrees, it needed the incident that happened at the Resia Pass.

After the American tanks had taken up positions along the road and the squads of infantrymen were deployed, we noticed across the border some infantry soldiers steadily coming our way. At a distance they first looked like Germans; as their pants were baggy and their uniforms appeared somewhat mixed but it soon became evident that they were fellow American soldiers.

As the group of them walked briskly towards us, one of them enthusiastically started running toward us. It was only then that I saw he was carrying what appeared to be a Speed Graphic still camera.

My God, I thought, he's an Army photographer.

We shook hands across the Italian-Austrian border. I recall he introduced himself as Corporal Weintraub of the 163rd Signal Photo Company and Don snapped our picture.

Not an earthshaking meeting but it was that which closed the circle of the American Army in Europe. The U.S. Seventh Army had marched all across Europe and there in the little town of Nauders in Austria, had finally linked up with the one who had started the whole fight in Italy three years before, General Mark Clark's small but courageous, Fifth Army.

Now that the circle had finally closed, I began to think of what my post-war life with Tina might be like and sought a means to return to her at long last.

Not long after our arrival, Don our driver, Jim Morris and I set up a small command post in an authentic Alpine farmhouse outside a small village just a few miles from the Austrian border. We were situated near a road junction which led to the city of Munster, Switzerland.

Our sleeping quarters were small, but overlooked a swiftly running fresh water stream. What struck our immediate curiosity was the very room itself with its high beamed ceilings covered with all sorts of hanging dry cured meats and cheeses. We saw enough food hanging from the ceiling over our heads to supply the needs of a small-sized town, let alone just one family who lived in the house we now shared.

The farmer spoke a German Tyrolese dialect and was a kindly middle-aged person about fifty years of age. He told us he was married, but he and his wife lived apart and we never had a chance to meet her.

He told us we could take from his alpine home any food that we wanted to. Don and I thanked him for his generosity and offered him what rations and supplies we could share.

It was quite clear that this single farmer who seemed more German than Italian, fared rather well during the German occupation than his countrymen to the south.

Don and I asked the farmer if he would share some of his fresh cream for our morning coffee. He presented us with a small silver pitcher of cream the very next morning and every morning after, so much so, we couldn't use it all. I unsuccessfully tried to explain to him that we still had cream from the previous day which we had kept chilled overnight on the windowsill in the cold evening mountain air. The very next morning there was always more. Don and I decided to share what we could of the cream with our fellow soldiers so we wouldn't hurt his feelings.

Don and I spent a considerable amount of time at the Swiss border talking with the guards, some of whom were quite fluent in English. We each swapped them some of our American cigarettes for their delicious chocolate.

After a while the Swiss guards Don and I had befriended allowed us to drive our jeep into the nearby border town of Munster which began all of about fifty yards away from the local border crossing.

Our Swiss hosts didn't consider our personal sightseeing expedition to be a significant breach of international law, since as a nation they had remained neutral through much of the war and general hostilities had now ended.

We enjoyed the opportunity we had been handed and it was only later while I was standing in a cigarette and candy store on the Swiss side of the border, that I actually entertained the pleasant thought myself of saying the hell with the Army on that day and just staying behind in Switzerland.

I had never honestly considered myself a possible deserter from the Army before, but I did then. I think my thoughts were more of an honest emotional response to fully recognizing for myself that the European war was largely over and I genuinely didn't want to go home.

The more I thought what kind of possible future I might enjoy with Tina after the war, the more I felt I urgently needed to find some means of remaining in Italy for as long as I could even if that decision meant volunteering to extend my enlistment in the U.S. Army.

I knew I had just willingly strayed across the Swiss border from our lines, and if I did remain there apart from my assigned unit and Don went back without me, what would happen to me?

Would I eventually be taken into custody by Army MPs, court-martialed and then discharged or would I be left alone?

I thought of Ernest Hemingway's novel, "A Farewell to Arms." I wondered to myself just how real fiction could become without blowing everything I valued to hell.

My impulsive thoughts to actually desert the Army on that day ended up being little more than escapist fantasies.

I would find another way to return to Italy and start a new life with Tina once I left the Army.

Chapter 17

Return to Merano

Merano, Italy

Garnay Wilson's tank outfit had overrun a German finance company somewhere in the Po Valley. The tankers had taken huge gunny sacks of counterfeit Italian lira which had been only recently printed by the Germans. The only visible difference between the original Italian money and the German issued currency lay in the small noticeable watermark seal found on each certificate.

These specific German bills were 1,000 lira notes and often referred to by the American GI's as wallpaper because of its large size. Most of these bills had been previously in circulation since the fall of Mussolini's government.

The recent Fifth Army advance had been so rapid throughout the Po Valley there was precious little time for the retreating Germans or the Italians themselves to allow for financial news to broadly circulate through the region which would have made these genuine-looking Italian lira bills utterly worthless.

Wilson and I took a couple of stacks of 1,000 lira notes into the city of Merano to see what we could pass among the local merchants, while it was still good, if it was at the time.

Merano, a well-known alpine ski resort could be described as a lush "city of flowers."

While Merano is completely surrounded by snowy peaks that can reach altitudes of 10,000 feet, the city itself sits in a lush valley only 1,000 feet high.

Judging that the Allied Military Government (AMG) had then established an exchange rate of 100 lira to a dollar, the two of us must have taken the equivalent of about $20,000 in U.S. dollars to the city of Merano to spend that single day.

Merano is also referred to by many Italians as the "citta ospedeliera," or city of hospitals. Because of its altitude and mild climate, the city had long been an ideal place to offer medical treatment towards curing many of the world's most crippling lung diseases. The region's curative mineral waters from nearby springs offered much relief before the start of the war to those who suffered from common stomach and intestinal disorders.

The most amazing part of our visit to Merano was that the city was still under a measure of general German administrative control. The only people we saw who filled the streets of the city when we first arrived were mostly German infantry soldiers and officers.

All of the traffic in the intersections within the city was controlled by well-disciplined German SS military policemen on motorcycles.

Garnay and I felt uneasy in our American-issue olive drab uniforms as we drove through the streets in our jeep. Each of us was the object of considerable German scrutiny, to say nothing of the few Italians who could not believe that we were there, knowing nothing of the overall military situation at this point.

The armistice between the German and Allied forces, even though it had just been settled, had not yet been publicly announced throughout the region.

It ran a little against the grain to see a German military policeman stop your American military vehicle and make you wait while some Mercedes open touring car full of Kraut brass slowly passed in front of you.

Wilson and I both agreed at that moment, that this was one hell of a way to win a war.

The two of us were busy walking around, casing the stores to see where we could best spend our money. While we were window shopping, an Italian eased up beside us and in true espionage fashion, asked if we were interested in some useful military information.

Since we were and had money even to pay, we agreed to follow him to a hospital nearby.

"In that clinic, there are some American soldiers," he said, in what I can describe as a rather sinister Peter Lorre type voice.

"I have a sister who works in the hospital. She told me those soldiers have been there for some time."

We each thanked our mysterious benefactor for his information, and he refused our offer of Italian lira for payment.

Garnay and I located the hospital the Italian had described. We walked through the front doors of the hospital clinic and asked a woman who greeted us if we could possibly be directed to the Americans who we believed were being treated there.

She immediately escorted us to a long pavilion full of hospital beds where in the middle of the ward we discovered eight, unmistakably young American infantry soldiers.

I saw at least some of the bed-ridden soldiers had full-length plaster casts on their legs and others had heavy white bandages wrapped around their chests, shoulders or heads.

They couldn't believe their eyes when they saw the two of us.

Wilson hit the bed of one of them and said loudly, "Okay guys, the honeymoon is over. It's back to your foxholes."

We heard a series of moans and groans and protests until we both began laughing. We then told them they were safe for the time being, but would probably be picked up by American forces soon.

They sighed with relief because, like the fighter pilots we encountered during our sightseeing tour of Venice, they were enjoying their holiday from the Army and the war.

In spite of their wounds and/or broken bones, they had been enjoying life in that place for a few months.

We asked them what they missed and, of course, cigarettes were on the top of their list. We got an orderly, an old man who spoke English, and told him to get whatever they wanted, even if it was prohibited.

We gave him a batch of bills that probably was more than he had seen in a year. We told the guys that we would be back with American cigarettes and candy, whatever we could get together from our task force.

As we went through the stores it became apparent to us that this section of Italy had not been raped and looted as the other parts of the country. The reason was obvious. The people spoke only German and were fully in sympathy with the Nazis, even though they were Italians.

The fact they had been under the rule of Italy since the First World War did not make them Italians. When we went into a store where there were Germans present, we were the last ones to be served and then they would speak to us only in German.

So whatever we wanted, we did by pointing and then letting them count off the amount of money required for its purchase.

Some of the shop owners were a little leery of the Italian currency we offered them. They probably wondered why the Americans had the same money as the Germans.

But then money was money and especially if they were getting more than double their price which I am sure they were. The two of us didn't care; we had more bundles of lira still to spend back in our jeep.

There wasn't too much merchandise offered for sale, but what there was, we bought it up to distribute among the guys in the task force.

We felt like real spoilers from ancient Roman times. But give or take, the money would eventually be taken up by the Italian government, so the shop owners would always come out on top.

We considered our effort a form of war reparations as far as the Italians were concerned.

We bought up cameras, film, food stuffs, liquors and wine. I purchased quite a lot of silk stockings with the idea that if I ever got back to Tina I would have a surprise for her since these fineries faded from the picture long ago in Florence.

To show what a small war it was, one day Don and I were in town and started talking to a young German military policeman. We discovered he spoke English very well.

We asked him where he had learned to speak English so well, and to our surprise, he said he once worked in an ice cream plant in Newark, New Jersey before the war.

Don said to him, "Perhaps you have heard of my father's place in Newark, Wiedenmayer's Ice Cream Company?"

The man's face lit up. "Wiedenmayer, mein Gott, that's where I worked. Mr. Wiedenmayer, is he your father? I cannot believe it!"

I could see there were tears welling in the German's eyes. He remembered Don as a young man when he worked there years before the war.

The young German had worked at the plant which had converted from making beer during Prohibition to making ice cream during the 1930s but left Newark when Adolph Hitler sent out the word requiring all Germans to return to their Fatherland.

He had heard of the propaganda, but admitted he still had family in Germany which he felt responsible for, and he thought he was doing the right thing by deciding to return home and serve in the German army.

Fortunately, because of his young age, he had never seen any real danger in combat against the Allies, and his one single desire was to return to New Jersey after the war when he could.

"One never gets too old," Don said to him, "to start life all over again."

Wilson handed Don and I a message which had been forwarded to us from the 196th Signal Photo Company headquarters which had recently been established in the nearby city of Verona.

The message required Don and I to go to German General Von Vietinghoff's headquarters, high up in the mountains near Bolzano.

Von Vietinghoff had taken over from Kesselring to defend the German Gothic Line when he had been recalled by Hitler to Germany.

The given reason for our mission was to locate all German photographic equipment and supplies in the immediate area and to arrange for their prompt turn-in to Fifth Army supply depots for appropriate disposition.

Don and I were directed to the location of a small village south of Bolzano where we would travel by a funicular train which would take us to German command headquarters on a high mountaintop across the valley. We each learned there was a road on the far side of the mountain we could take to the peak, but it wasn't considered passable at the time.

We made copies of our order at headquarters to show to the Germans before we boarded the train.

Don and I stepped inside the train car with one German soldier cradling a Schmeisser.

We were likewise armed but the situation still gave each of us butterflies to be up some 2,000 feet in the air with a German who spoke no English and looked every bit as sinister as he seemed.

For the first time, Don said something funny, which really broke the tension.

He looked down at the never-ending valley below and then at the German soldier in the car.

"Burke," he said, "I can see it all now."

"We get half way across; this guy blows our heads off and shoves us out."

"You think we are going over there for some motion picture film? You want to know the truth; I think we are going to be the feature of the week."

I looked back at the German to see if he understood any of what we were saying. He muttered something unintelligible in German which didn't seem to mean anything of consequence to either of us.

I looked across the car at Don and said, "If you're going to have a name like Wiedenmayer, you should at least know some German, if we're going to make it safely to the other side."

Don returned a smile towards me in recognition of my point.

Each of us kept the palm of our hands close enough to our holsters for the duration of the crossing just to play it safe.

I think that ride across the valley gave me an everlasting hang-up about funicular trains.

Every time I've been on one since then, I have always had a feeling that someone was going to cut the cables or that the car would get stuck, making a hanging rope escape necessary.

The fear I felt was real, and I still feel nervous any time I've been in a gondola suspended in open space by a piece of thin cable.

We were accompanied from the station below up to General Vietinghoff's command headquarters in a large, mountain-style fortress building of heavy wood and stone. The mountaintop retreat was surrounded by large trees and secured by what looked like a platoon of armed, attentive German infantry. The Germans had reason to be on alert since they had experienced an Italian partisan attack only a couple of weeks before.

The orderly at the main entrance did not speak English but was attentive to our presence and immediately took us to a German officer down the hall. Don and I walked under a heavy beamed ceiling as we looked out through massive clear glass windows which overlooked the surrounding valley. Everything we saw throughout the entire residence, from furnishings to fixtures was immaculate.

The German officer, who greeted us, examined our orders, looked squarely at each of us, forced a smile, and then politely excused himself to enter a nearby office.

After a moment, he returned.

"You may go in now," he said.

As we started to move, he quickly added, "Without your guns, of course."

When he saw us hesitate a moment, he said, "They will be quite safe here, I assure you."

We took off our weapons and went into the office. It was an extremely large and comfortable room.

Its furnishings were heavy and numerous yet there was a measure of intimacy about it. It was a room that obviously had the same occupant for quite some time, judging from the collective mementos then scattered about the large room.

The German officer seated behind the desk was an older man and quite handsome. An attractive blonde woman in her late forties stood near him. Her manner of dress reminded me for the moment of Tina, who often wore a favorite camel cashmere sweater with a matching cardigan over it.

A handsome, dark-haired gentleman with a large, full-moustache in civilian clothes observed us but didn't speak. I suspected from his manner he was Italian and possibly Sicilian.

The German officer seated behind the desk went over the content of the orders he had prepared. He did not offer that we sit down.

"So you want to get our photographic equipment and all our motion picture film. What do you expect to do with it?"

"What my Army expects to use it for is their business," I said.

"We are only here to find out where the material is and to get you to authorize its release," I began.

"When we know where it is, I will pass along the information to my superiors who will then organize its collection. The process will all be legal and done in the appropriate manner.

"We're all alike. We have our orders and have to follow them," He replied dryly.

He then depressed the toggle button of a telephone switchboard situated on his desk.

Lights flickered and he began talking to someone in rapid and officious German.

The blonde woman came over to me.

"Tell me, is it true that you bombed Capri and it is now destroyed?"

The situation made Don and I laugh a little.

"Don't tell me you believe your own propaganda. No, Capri is still there and just as beautiful as ever. Our soldiers now use the city as a rest area," I said.

"I loved it so much. We spent a lot of time there," she said.

When she said "we" she glanced towards the dark man.

Obviously the "we" meant the two of them.

"I will return there when this is all over. I may even live there," she said.

"You could have picked worse places, I agree. It's quite a place."

The German officer had finished talking on the phone and hung up the receiver.

"I am issuing you orders from me authorizing you to collect all photographic equipment and film that we currently have in headquarters at Trento for disposition. You will do so under German supervision.

I will have this typed for you while you wait."

I took out a pack of cigarettes and offered them. They all took one.

Don didn't smoke.

"I suppose you American photographers have a great deal of admiration for our Leica cameras, eh?"

"They can be beat. But you have something that can't, and that's the Arriflex camera. It might just be your best hope you have in peacetime Germany. That and the little Volkswagen jeep," I told him. "I understand you had a raid on this headquarters, a short time ago."

"It happened just about two weeks ago. Those damned partisans came in from the other side. Altogether, there were about forty of their people killed here. It was really stupid on their part."

"I would imagine you would find it pretty safe way up here like this."

"Well, that was the idea. But when you are losing, even the dogs are biting at your heels."

It was well for him to say but I didn't see any dogs around his well-shined boots.

The papers he had ordered prepared for us were soon produced and handed to Don and I.

"I hope you will find everything in order at the photo section. If there is any problem, you do know where to reach me."

It was funny. He said it like he was going to pass the rest of his life there. It was only a question of days before he and all the rest of the remaining Germans now comfortably living in the mountaintop retreat would be jammed together in some prisoner of war compound as all the others.

I thanked him. We then shook hands and left. Outside, Don and I picked up our weapons and again walked down the same long hallway from where we came.

The steady sound of our clicking boot heels echoed throughout the place.

When Don and I arrived back at the nearby task force command post, we dispatched the German papers through the 10th Mountain Division headquarters to forward to our own unit commander, Major Linden Rigby, at 196th Signal Photo Company headquarters, wherever in hell that actually was at that time. I knew some American courier would eventually find it.

Apparently, Major Rigby did, because Don and I discovered all of the German photo equipment found at Trento had been properly turned over to the 196th Signal Photo Company as it had been directed. All of the motion picture film that had been shot by German motion picture combat photographers had been relegated to history.

Maybe generations from now, someone will think to thank photographers on both sides that filmed the European war so future generations will have a chance to experience what it was like to serve in the Second World War.

Not long after our most recent adventure, Don and I received new orders assigning us to drive to a location near Lake Garda where a large German prisoner of war camp was being established at Ghedi Airfield.

If you think of the more than twenty-six divisions the Germans had in the field opposing us spread across the Po Valley and up in the Alps which now had surrendered, you can visualize an extensive prisoner of war compound.

So Don, our driver Jim and I packed up our camera gear and headed off towards Riva along Lake Garda for a first stop.

Word quickly spread to disregard any Italian lira without the correct watermark of the king on the bottom circle. The stacks of money we had held became worthless wallpaper.

It was a shame to have to turn your back on what had once been about $100,000 in actual Italian currency, but at least we had the personal satisfaction of having spent at least some of it.

Chapter 18

War's end

Riva, Lake Garda, May 1945

Riva is a small resort town situated at the northern end of Lake Garda in the Po Valley.

Don and I had planned on spending only a single night near Riva, but discovered a pleasant reason to extend our stay.

Soldiers at the 10th Mountain Division headquarters had filled an entire sports stadium with crates of liquor they had taken from the Germans.

When the two of us arrived at the stadium we could not believe what we saw. The stadium's oval cinder track was a giant drive-in liquor store. Neatly-stacked cases of every kind of wine, whiskey, cognac, champagne or whatever you could drink was on hand. The whole scene looked like an Army ration dump. It was the largest collection of drinking material I had ever seen before in my life.

Two G.I.s stood guard, and Don introduced himself to them in order to take pictures for their home town newspapers. I also rolled off a few feet of newsreel film capturing the same scene.

The guys running this liquor supply dump were delighted to be photographed posed sitting on top of mountains of vintage French champagne.

The scene resembled a recovering alcoholic's nightmare.

If the Allies had been smart, we could have given the Germans sufficient time to drink all of that stuff and then taken them over easily in a drunken stupor.

The two Army infantrymen on duty were more interested in having their picture taken by Don than to observe our driver, Jim carefully making his way through the aisles to select only the best brands and then tucking his booty neatly away in our canvas-covered equipment trailer.

Don and I finished taking photos and were preparing to leave, when the same two soldiers came up to us in low whispered tones and said, "If you guys would like to have a bottle of cognac, it can be arranged."

I looked across the jeep at Jim our driver.

He had to turn the other way from the two infantrymen as to not reveal his laughter.

"Us, take a bottle of cognac?" I asked them.

"It's very great of you to offer it but you see, we never drink while we're in uniform. Thanks just the same. It's quite a collection you got there and it was fun seeing it."

With that, we took our leave.

As we were riding back towards Riva, I recall Don leaned forward and asked Jim, "How much did you get?"

"Let's just say that I left some of it. We got enough, Don, we got enough," he laughingly replied.

Our jeep passed a local post office which appeared to be open. We observed a line of local people waiting in line and I went over to investigate.

What I found gave me a pleasant surprise.

The Italian postal service was now back in operation for the first time between the northern and southern parts of Italy.

It didn't take me a minute to make up my mind. I got out a letter writing folder I always kept with me and wrote a short letter to Tina. I had no idea when the letter might ever arrive at the villa. Addressing the letter to her would relieve some of the deep despair I had felt throughout the Fifth Army's fast-moving campaign north while I had been apart from her.

I told her where I now was in Riva, how much I loved her, where I had been and what the prospects appeared to be of my ever seeing her again.

The letter was a voice in the wilderness, sounding off into space, hoping to be heard.

I put a generous amount of Italian stamps on the letter, probably enough to get it to the North Pole and back. I reasoned that if the extra stamps would somehow speed my message to Tina, then the cost would be well worth it.

We resumed our drive towards the Brescia Airfield, near Desenzano, situated a little south of Lake Garda. The sprawling facility was an ex-military airport bordered by wrecked aircraft, both Italian and German around it. The operation of the prisoner of war camp was being handled by the Japanese-American 442nd Regimental Combat Team (RCT).

Don and I stayed with the Tullio Ferreri family in Desenzano while we worked on the Fifth Army Concentration Area story. We each wanted to work in different places—and we only had one jeep. Don went to the nearby motor pool and got a camouflaged German Mercedes to use. During his drive to and from Desenzano, Don was booed by the local Italian kids. He forgot the car had German markings.

Coils of barbed wire were strung around the perimeter, and inside the compound designated service areas, sanitary facilities and messing space were set apart.

As the German prisoners came in, still commanded by their own officers and enlisted non-commissioned officers, they were stripped of all personal possessions they had. All of their personal belongings, money, letters and the like, were put in a sealed envelope accurately identified by name. All types of military equipment they brought in with them were also taken away from them by their captors.

I immediately put in a special request to my superiors that all German photographic equipment being turned in be earmarked for the Army Pictorial Service.

Surprisingly enough, Don and I discovered quite a few combat photographers among the prisoners. Their cameras were superb, especially the Arriflex model which I had used in North Africa. They parted with them unwillingly and I couldn't blame them.

The Germans, for the majority, had surrendered in company-sized units or larger. These units were kept intact and were brought to the camp using their own available transportation. Complete units were housed together and remained led by their own officers.

If any of them had any ideas about being given American rations, cigarettes and whatever, it was soon dispelled when they saw their own trailer type of field kitchen pull up to their area. They lined up to eat their usual gravy-like goulash and sauerkraut and black bread, which tasted like half-sawdust.

So long as available German food rations held out, that would be their bill of fare.

Over on the Brescia Airport's concrete runways large shower units were set up along with disinfectant stations. The entire compound held something like 150,000 prisoners and the security task was enormous. The Allies set up the facility quickly and it worked efficiently.

Even the Germans seemed to be happy in their new surroundings, but then I guess if you had been in the field for as many years as they had, anything different was a welcome, positive change.

I had my Bell and Howell Eyemo motion picture camera set up with a 400-foot magazine on a tripod in the rear of our jeep. I asked Jim to drive slowly so that I could take a smooth travel shot of the entire prisoner of war compound. We each suddenly heard a funny noise followed by a loud hissing sound.

The Germans heard it too, and quickly hit the ground. We had just run over some iron pieces cemented into the former runway that had been only recently cut off with a cutting torch. The jagged metal ends had ripped out two right-side tires of our jeep.

Jim and I headed over to the maintenance section run by soldiers of the Japanese-American 442nd Regimental Combat Team. We needed tires but they had none to spare.

It was odd that I was then suddenly thinking of Tina at that time, because all of a sudden something urgently clicked in my mind. I remembered an Italian tire plant taken over by the Army located not far from Tina's family home that was now actively re-treading military tires for our forces.

I saw a perfect chance to see Tina once again, and I knew I might not get another precious opportunity like this for quite some time, if at all.

After all, Don and I did need tires for our jeep. I mentioned this to the sergeant in charge of the maintenance section and he agreed with the urgency of the situation.

Just to make the whole mission legal, I had the maintenance sergeant sign a pick-up supply order for five tires in exchange for ours.

He not only signed the supply request, but added a few more tires to the order for himself.

I told my partner, still photographer Don Wiedenmayer when I saw him at the airfield that the trip to the tire re-treading plant was strictly a supply mission and that only our driver Jim and I would go since we needed the room to carry back the extra tires when we returned.

Don seemed perfectly content to remain behind and continue to take still photographs of newly-arriving German prisoners.

Jim and I left, driving on with borrowed tires, hoping to make the villa before dark.

The trip south towards Florence was much lonelier, and at times spookier than usual. While traveling south, we had to pass by all manner of burned out German tanks and vehicles, some of them still partially blocking the road we traveled. Dead horses and livestock were scattered where they fell, and local Italian farmers were busy doing their part in getting them properly buried before a real disease epidemic could spread throughout the region.

The countryside we traveled through was noticeably bare of life as far as the American armed forces that were now in control were concerned. American military policemen guarded bridges and other important crossings as necessary.

It was late in the afternoon when we hit the Apennine mountains on Route 64 which was the more direct route going to the villa. I had told Jim that we had to be through the mountains before nightfall. The aftermath of any war is the same. Modern-day carpetbaggers passing themselves off as Partisans or displaced persons were actively robbing, stealing and killing for black market profits. During that time, with the war just ended, desperate people wanted material goods, not Italian currency, which they knew had become worthless.

So Allied jeeps, tires, gas, weapons and clothing were premium items and the price of a human life meant little or nothing in order to acquire them.

Jim and I had made an understanding at the beginning of the mountains, not to stop for anything or anybody. When we met an American weapons carrier trying to navigate a sharp turn coming towards us in the opposite direction we nearly clipped him on the side.

Jim heard me say, "Screw him," and with that, he jammed his foot down on the gas. That was no place to stop and argue who then had the right of way.

I had thought many times about how it would be meeting Tina once again after being away for so long.

Before the spring offensive, we enjoyed a temporary dating arrangement. But after having left Tina, and then coming back to find her once again, it was as though everything had passed and that the present would now be forever. I felt as if our battle of farewells had been won.

I was standing on a little knoll near the villa, looking down toward the meadow. An excited Lucia had told me that Tina and Rina had taken a walk down there late in the afternoon.

I saw them coming across the little bridge over the creek. For a moment I just stood there to see what their reaction would be.

For a while, they didn't seem to even see me. Then all of a sudden, they both let out screams and ran toward me.

I grabbed Tina up in my arms with a strength that should have broken her ribs. I could hear her saying, "Gatto, Gatto, you have come back. You're here! But for how long?"

I said to her, "Hey, not so fast. Come on, we'll go inside and I'll tell you all."

I kissed Rina and told her that I had not seen John since the last time we were here together. I knew how she felt. Her sad round face looked up at me. She was wondering if I could come, then so could John.

But I explained that it was not so. We were all assigned to different photo sections and I had a different partner now.

Just by chance I had the problem with the tires; otherwise I could not have come.

Tina said that someone was not only watching over us and arranging our meetings, but was watching over the jeep as well.

"Of course," I said. "Without that jeep, I'd be like a man without legs. Then it would be really tough to try and get to see you."

The days were beginning to be warm but in the evening a warm fireplace was needed. Tina and I talked and drank and enjoyed our dinner meal, and then talked some more.

We each knew there was so much to say, to hear, to ask and to know.

Signore Raffaello had wanted to know all about the Germans and what they ever did with all the animals they had stolen from him. When I told him they never got across the Po River, he laughed and said something like "serves those bastards right for stealing them."

Since those animals, stranded in the valley, were obviously from this area, I suggested that he write a letter to the American Military Government in Florence to ask for either payment for the missing livestock, or replacements from the herds stranded up north.

I gave Tina, Rina, and her father, Signore Raffaello all of the goodies I had purchased earlier in Merano with the phony Italian money I had found. It had been a long time since Tina had seen silk stockings; they had practically gone out of style.

I gave her father two unblocked Borsalino hats. I told Tina about the letter I had mailed to her from Merano but she hadn't yet received it. Who knows, I thought, when and if the letter I had written would ever be delivered.

I heard the sad news of how the family dog, poor Giovacchino had become an innocent victim of the war. He was standing near as one of the Army transportation soldiers was busy chopping wood for Beppa. One block of wood being split slipped away, and the ax swung wildly away from the soldier using it, and hit the dog on the head. Tina thought the family dog might recover from the injury, but later died from convulsions.

Jim Morris, our driver, left me behind and drove our jeep early the next morning to the tire re-treading plant on his own.

Tina, Rina and I prepared a picnic lunch and went down into the meadow near the villa. We all enjoyed a walk and a leisurely lunch and later laid down in the heavy clover field looking up into the clear blue sky. The air that day was cool and crisp, and filled with the scent of spring.

Nearby, the hunters were shooting at the returning migratory birds that now swooped down over the little lake that had been built there long ago by the Medicis.

It seemed so impossible that all this should ever end. Our hands met amid the thick foliage. Rina was on her knees busily hunting for four-leafed clovers.

Tina leaned over toward me.

"What do you think will happen now that the war is over? Where will you go?"

I rose up on my elbows.

"The Army has taken over Trieste and that part near Yugoslavia. Then there's a photo section that's going into Austria with a possible headquarters in Vienna. I was thinking that if I could get into one or the other, it wouldn't be too far from you."

"I want to speak frankly and I want to be honest," Tina said. It seemed that it was difficult for her to say the words.

"Burke, people have fallen in love during wartime before. They all make promises, or try to. I don't want you to do something that may affect your life. You are, after all, an American and have your family at home."

"My country yes, but my family, well . . . we've been so far apart for so long."

I continued, "But I do have my mother. Let me say this. I have fallen in love with you and I want you. Now, how that comes about is another story." I looked deep into Tina's eyes,

"Do you want me as much as I want you, in the same way?"

"Yes; I do," Tina said. "I do not want to make your life any more complicated. Let's see each other as much as we can, and when we can. After that, maybe our protectors will decide for us."

I told her, "Our protectors haven't been doing too badly so far. Do you realize that we've been going together for ten months? We'll have an anniversary soon."

"And I'll have a birthday, too."

It was a funny thing, but until then, I never had asked her when her birthday was.

"It will be July 10th."

"We'll have a party. I'll be here no matter where the Army sends me."

"I'll be here as well, my love."

I turned my head up towards the pale blue sky.

"Do you hear that, protectors, July 10, 1945—and I've got to be here. Make sure you arrange that. It's a date. July 10th." I leaned over and pressed my lips gently onto hers.

That night we danced and listened to our favorite records which we had played over and over so many times before. We held each other close as Bing Crosby crooned one of her favorite songs, "Amour."

Tina had always wanted me to write the lyrics of that song for her. The song was her favorite and I guess, as time went by, it became mine. I played the record a little, then stopped it, wrote down a few verses, and started the recording once again until I had written down all of the words.

Our good friend, Rina went to bed and left us alone.

Tina and I didn't want to go to bed because that would mean that the night was over and we wanted the evening to go on forever.

It was late when we went out into the garden. Everything seemed so still. No more were there reflections behind the mountains of the distant Allied artillery. No planes droned overhead and there were small lights all around the countryside, indicating the return of normal life to the small homes and villages in Tuscany.

The Transportation Company had long since moved out and the land their trucks occupied seemed immensely empty. We stood there, tightly embraced, one against the other.

I remember the first time I walked into her garden. The 25-pounders were blasting away. Now there was a stillness that was almost frightening. Time had come and now it had gone. Only the echoes of war remained.

Tina looked up at me. "What are you thinking about?"

"Just about you; it seems that everything I think of ends up with you. Let's go in. It's getting late."

The large cathedral-like wooden door made a rumbling noise as I slammed it shut. After that, all was quiet and the night was still.

We arrived back at the POW compound in the afternoon. I had a good feeling about having seen Tina and to reassure her that there would always be time for us. But whatever thoughts I might have had concerning another quick return visit, were smashed to bits when I saw Don Wiedenmayer running up to meet us.

"Hey Burke. You're back just in time." Don was tall and youthful and his manner of speaking was almost breathless. "We just received some great news."

I could not even try to imagine what great news he could have received.

"Okay Don, you've got my interest. Now what's so great?"

"We're being called back to company. We're going back to the States; the war is over for us. Here, read the message."

I took the paper that he offered. It wasn't long but very terse and to the point. We were to cease all photographic activities at once and return to the company headquarters in Verona.

Don was like a schoolboy who was just promoted. "Isn't that terrific, Burke? Now we can get the hell out of here and go back to the good old USA."

I didn't share his enthusiasm. "Yeah, that's just terrific, Don, terrific."

It was not the thing to feel but right then I almost hated him for his prep school enthusiasm. I wanted to tell him to go back to Newark and leave me alone. He had always talked about his girl there. Sure, he wanted to get back. Many of them did, but they weren't leaving something they had learned to care for. Such a change would leave many American GI's with mixed emotions, but not the likes of Don. He would go back to warm family life that he left a few years before. The hovering family affection, the grand welcome from friends, of course for him, it would be great. That would be really terrific.

My thoughts flashed across my mind. Would I arrive at Grand Central Station, or would it be the Pennsylvania Station?

Maybe I would enjoy a few drinks in the bar with the guys who would probably be with me.

Then they would be off to their families in the Bronx or Brooklyn and I would go off to some reasonable hotel, maybe the Taft. Then I'd start looking for some small, furnished apartment I could afford after three years and nine months in the Army.

Yes Don, really terrific. But the indifference I felt for him at that moment was nothing more than a way of not facing up to the facts as they were. Maybe there was also a little envy in the back of my mind.

My thoughts were of Tina. What they did with me was the Army's business, but I didn't want to get her hurt. But then I should have thought of that months before. We were both committed now and our life was slipping from our grasp. There would be nothing we could do about it. I wondered if they would let me go and see her for one last farewell, but I knew that was stupid. The Army does not have that kind of foresight.

From Verona they could ship us out through Venice or even Trieste, making it completely impossible for me to see Tina ever again.

I guess many of us had come to accept the war and the Army as a way of life. It just kept going on and on. It was almost four years, and three-fourths of that was overseas.

The sudden thought of having to return home was leaving me utterly unprepared. It was an adjustment I had not thought of making; at least, not then.

But then as I was deep in thought, I felt a growing urgency in my stomach, like I had felt many times before when we had to move up. It was like something was waiting to happen, to happen to me. Maybe it was time to go. Maybe at Verona there would be something unexpected. Something might happen. It had to happen. I knew it. I felt it.

I looked at Jim and Don. "Well guys, if they want us back, then our war stops here. Let's pack and we'll leave tomorrow morning. Who knows what strange things may be lurking in the dark for us in Verona. How was it in the Shakespearean play, 'Two Gentlemen from Verona?' Or was it three? To hell with it, let's go."

Chapter 19

Garrison duty in Verona

By mid-May 1945, the war in Europe had largely come to an end for the officers and men of the 196th Signal Company who received orders from the far reaches of the Po Valley from their Captain Ned R. Morehouse, their commanding officer to report to unit headquarters established in a three-story apartment building in a suburb of the ancient city of Verona, familiar as the setting for William Shakespeare's plan, Romeo and Juliet.

Verona, Italy 1945

The city of Verona, Italy is situated in a loop of the Adige River near Lake Garda and home to the Ponti de Pietra, one of the few Roman bridges that managed to successfully survive the war.

The 196th Signal Photo Company had established its primary field headquarters upon its arrival on April 28, 1945 in a modest residential building, and nearby, a cluster of buildings had in short order, been quickly transformed into a crisp, efficient, military headquarters compound, of which any American soldier then arriving could certainly be proud.

It must be deeply instilled somewhere deep in the heart of our Army brass, "if it moved, salute it; if it doesn't move, pick it up; if you can't pick it up, at least try to paint it white."

The modest exterior of the building was protected by thick coils of new steel barbed wire except for a closely guarded front entrance. An armed MP checked our identification papers and signaled us through.

Why all of this intense security was actually necessary, I could never figure out.

Our new headquarters was being run strictly "by the book" and new, neatly painted signs directed Don and I to the company motor pool, the orderly room, the nearby mess hall, supply and wherever else our boss thought might be helpful.

The more carefully stenciled military signs were nailed in place, the generally more shaped up the area must have looked.

Headquarters had survived its war years doing exactly just this sort of thing, and now they were ready to begin the process to trim its ranks down to size for redeployment to the Pacific war.

Don and I were told to unpack our personal gear and then to turn in our assigned jeep and trailer to the nearby motor pool.

Next, came return and check in of our side arms and all ammunition Don and I had carried for over three years of enlisted military service, and then each of our still and motion picture cameras and supplies. Everything else that we might have had in our custody which once had been considered government property was turned in and taken away.

Each of us walked in to the unit's personnel office, stated our names, and signed the unit's official roster as if we were first checking in as inmates in a local county jail. Neither one of us was any longer an independent Army photographer, but reduced to just another neatly typed last name, on a long list of other similarly-typed last names which was so long that I recall that it took me ten minutes of shuffling through the complete roster, even though my last name began with the letters "O'C" until I actually found it.

Don Wiedenmayer expressed considerable delight to be back in garrison once more, and it wasn't long before we headed off for lunch in the nearby mess hall.

I stood alone in the open field area outside the main entrance of our garrison compound after lunch and looked at the crisp, military order which now surrounded me. We were now creatures of the Army's daily routine as the once wild and free life we enjoyed in the field had at last come to an end.

Our arrival in Verona marked the beginning of summer, and the hot, dry June heat felt good against my skin. I felt in a noticeable way I had been freshly castrated as all the things I had carried around, worked with, cared for over the past three years, which had become an integral part of my life as a soldier, were now suddenly gone.

Other arriving soldiers said they preferred the relative comfort of Army garrison life to the field.

On post, a soldier had few, real responsibilities, and nearly everything was neatly provided for by the Army without as much as one even lifting a finger.

I had always preferred taking my chances in combat against the Germans, and to be away from the sheer suffocation of headquarters.

But there I was.

I was now confined, facing a very good chance of standing kitchen (KP) duties, and the prospect of participating in hours of close order drill once again staring me in the face.

I wondered, quietly to myself, what the hell was my future going to be now?

How long would we be here?

Would I ever be able to get a pass to leave headquarters to see the village of Colli Alti to see Tina ever again, or celebrate her birthday as I hoped I would?

I surveyed the miserable situation I now found myself in, and saw no possible exit from that endless tunnel now facing me.

If it had been true that someone "up there" was acting like a divine force who guided our lives, then they would have to start working overtime because the present situation was getting too normal, and too screwed up at the moment.

Little by little, the warring heroes of the 196th Signal Photo Company finally returned from their assigned fields of battle in Northern Italy.

It was funny to see us all together. There weren't two enlisted soldiers in the whole unit who dressed alike.

I ran out to meet my good friend, John Mason who was by then arriving with his partner, fellow photographer Staff Sgt. Dave Kurland. It seemed like months since I had seen John and just being with him once again made me feel less lonely and less sympathetic with myself.

"Gee kid, you look great. A little thin though," John quipped when he saw me.

"But I guess Don couldn't cook as well as Beppa," he said as we walked toward the barracks.

Don Wiedenmayer recalls he wasn't offered an opportunity by Burke to travel to the Villa Calamai during the final months of the war while the two men worked together. Upon learning the story of Burke and Tina's wartime relationship and what his life was like at the Villa Calamai, he wishes Burke had told him more.

My stepfather chose to keep his relationship with Tina Calamai entirely private from Don Wiedenmayer throughout the time they worked together. The two men did enjoy a great working relationship and friendship both in the field and during their remaining time together at 196th Signal Company headquarters in Verona.

The two men enjoyed a great working friendship in the field in the latter months of the war which continued when they returned together to 196th Signal Company headquarters in Verona.

Burke chose to renew his earlier friendship with his first partner, John Mason after his arrival in Verona, and Don recalls seeing much less of him on a daily basis before the unit returned to the United States.

"Where the hell have you guys been?"

"You know the war ended a little while back."

Kurland was first to reply.

"To tell you the truth, Burke, we were holed up near Ivrea and then we spent a lot of time in Torino."

John soon joined in.

"Yeah, we each went through the Olivetti typewriter plant."

"Did you bring home any samples?"

"Two each," Kurland added. "We sent them home."

John and I later went upstairs where we had left our personal gear to be unpacked and set up our sleeping cots near one another.

As we each unpacked, I filled in John on the most recent trip I'd made to the villa at Colli Alti.

"Poor Rina; she really missed you, John."

"I know. Don't think I haven't been missing the hell out of her. You know Burke; she's one hell of a girl."

John leaned closer and said in a quiet voice, "How are we ever going to break out of this regimentation and get back there? Christ, without wheels, we're stuck."

"I don't know, Johnny, but I've got to work out something. And it had better be fast, too."

"It will have to be fast because I don't think they are going to keep us around here for too long. I guess we will just have to play it by ear and see what happens."

Headquarters didn't take long to transform all of us into real garrison type soldiers. Newly-issued, fresh khaki uniforms had replaced our old battle-worn ODs.

I reluctantly gave up my old, well-worn, combat boots that had carried me over so many miles. In return, I received a pair of new beige color boots that had the leather reversed so the outside was a rough finish.

John looked at his and said, "How about that, kid, suede boots."

"John, these boots are supposed to wear better in the sand than the smooth finish we've been wearing. I think they are trying to prepare us for the Pacific."

"Hey come on, not even joking."

There wasn't much for us to do. John and I swapped stories and exchanged souvenirs.

In a way, it was fun for all of us in the unit to finally be together once again. We were all in harmony with each other. We had always been a divided lot with the "company".

We passed our time playing cards, watching screenings of motion picture footage others had taken in the field, and some popular movies shipped in from back in the States.

Most of us discovered a small, nearby wine tavern, and passed more than a few dollars of our Army pay sampling their best Bardolino and Soave wines.

It was something that always struck me as being odd, that with all the drinking and stealing by the armies, the general wine supply throughout Italy was always high, including potent grappa, no matter where we traveled. Maybe there was just no telling how much of the stuff they really made up from one year to another.

You had to be a well-seasoned drinker to drink large quantities of grappa and still know how to find your way home to your barracks cot when you finally did make it home.

One day, Lt. Frank Morang called a general meeting of all photographic personnel. Morang served in the dual roles of Corps photo officer for II Corps and he was also our personnel officer.

We were soon told that all still and motion picture photographers with the least amount of service in the 196th Signal Photo Company faced possible reassignment to Trieste or Austrian commands.

Those of us with longer overseas enlisted service would return to the U. S. and be given a thirty months' leave before redeploying to the Pacific war with our unit.

Many of us with much longer time in service asked that we be assigned to a list of military photographic personnel scheduled to remain in Europe if at all possible.

I considered the request a long shot, but one I thought might keep me nearer to Tina for at least a little while longer after the war.

Our own former Commanding Officer, Colonel Melvin E. Gillette, who had left the Fifth Army during the winter, had by then been assigned by the War Department as Chief Photo Officer for the Pacific with headquarters in the Philippine capital of Manila. He had personally earmarked all of "his boys" to join him. This would mean that we were being invited to a beach party to be held on the sands of Japan.

That night, with our overall morale dragging behind us, and the prospect of Japan a real possibility, a group of us went to our favorite wine tavern in Verona and drank glass after glass of grappa and sometimes chased down each with a generous glass of Soave.

Most of us also ate a lot of pickled vegetables and hard salami. By the time we all finished that evening, we convinced the locals we rugged Americans could handle grappa, just like a proud Italian native.

One difference the Verona locals didn't have to contend with was having to find their way home to a strange barracks bunk in the dark without awakening one of the early to bed "company" boys. Thankfully, I staggered home to my bunk that evening without much notice.

The late night air was hot and sticky and the whole miserable atmosphere gave me a massive wave of claustrophobia. I couldn't stop thinking anxiously about Tina.

I fought back my fears that my unit, the 196th SPC might be officially whisked out of Italy without too much notice.

God, I thought, if only I had a jeep, or some form of transportation. I'd have to find some way to take off to the villa to see Tina before it was too late.

But without wheels, I was just stuck.

"Hey up there," I thought, "God, what are you planning?"

With my eyes toward the Heavens, I added, "It's got to be something quick, before they get me on the way to Japan. I'm leaving it up to you. I did what I could when I had the power. But now they have reduced me to a number with nothing left."

I was thinking about my heavenly protectors when the full measure of all the Italian grappa I drank that evening rapidly took me off into the slumbering arms of Morpheus.

I was half asleep and yet, half awake. It must have been early in the morning when I felt the first immediate sharp pain hit me.

Suddenly, I wasn't dreaming.

No, it was the time I was ambushed, and the Germans shot me in the ass . . . no, that wasn't it.

I never did get shot . . . what was it then . . . something's hit me in the ass . . . I know, I'm in the hospital and they gave me a shot . . . for malaria . . . no, I'm not dreaming . . . it hurts too much not to be real.

My eyelids gradually relaxed into a semi-open position. The barracks room still was filled with sleeping hulks under GI-issued blankets.

I rolled over to my side. Intense pain shot through my ass down to my groin and into my legs. I reached over behind me to find out what had hit me. I felt and found a swelling from my rear end the size of an egg and it was clearly hurting and throbbing like hell.

It was hemorrhoids!

Christ, what a time to get a thing like hemorrhoids!

I had been lucky against the Germans and their crack shots all throughout the war and now this!

I got up and quickly dressed myself as best I could. I could hardly walk, and each and every immediate bending movement made the throbbing, burning pain coming from my ass even more acute.

I thought of going to the bathroom but the mere thought alone sent shudders and chills all over me. I headed downstairs and found the kitchen staff already on the job preparing to serve hot coffee.

I suddenly felt like taking a large bucket of hot, steaming coffee and sitting my ass in it.

It was still early morning, but at least I knew I'd be the first to sign the sick call book if I could get there.

Army doctors generally have the idea that a typical soldier-patient knows all about his particular illness.

They always start their inquiry with, "Well, where did you get this?"

I told him that if I knew, I would sure as hell give it back. An infantryman comes in with a slug in his shoulder and the doctor says, "Hey, you've been shot."

After the Army treating physician had stuck, what seemed like his whole arm up my ass, he turned to me with a grave expression.

"Well, I'm going to tell you what you are up against. Number one, if you go to the hospital, they will operate. It's one hell of an operation, I can tell you. After that, it's no telling where you might end up. If you are on a list to go home, then I say to nurse it along and maybe it will retract."

Going to a hospital was about the last thing I certainly wanted to do at that time.

I'd try almost anything before that.

The doctor gave me a generous supply of ointment and powder he told me to dissolve in a tub of very hot water and then sit in it. After treating my sore bottom with the ointment, I'd have to try to push and shove the lump back up inside.

I felt horrible just thinking about the treatment, let alone doing it myself.

In an unusual situation like this one, I was, for the moment, fully immobilized, and knew I would have to quickly get well as soon as possible.

My illness gave my fellow photographers something they could each laugh about.

I was also rather fond of Italian bathrooms equipped with a bidet, without which, I could never have made my treatment as effective.

Surprisingly, the hideous lump soon began to retreat and progressively got smaller and smaller in size. It wasn't long before the entire lump was gone.

I couldn't believe it. A proud wave of personal accomplishment suddenly came over me.

Not only had I cured myself of that terrible pain, but now I was back in shape for whatever might afford me another chance to see Tina.

Little did I know at that moment in my recovery, it was to be my case of hemorrhoids themselves which would actually do the trick.

Fate, or whoever it was up there now pulling the strings for me, certainly moved in strange ways, but I guess there is never any measure of true joy in life without suffering a measure of personal pain along the journey.

The 703rd Engineers began construction of a four-inch, double pipeline carrying vital gasoline to the Fifth Army front soon after the capture of the port of Livorno. By November 23, 1944, the pipeline had reached Highway 65 just a few miles behind the winter lines. Burke and John Mason were assigned by Fifth Army Photo Officer Major Linden R. Rigby to photograph the completion of this project to the front lines. While working on the assignment, the pair resided at the Villa Calamai outside of Florence.
—*Photo by John T. Mason, 196th Signal Photo Company, February 1945
111-MM 45 22358 (National Archives)*

"Pipeline walkers" used military jeeps to inspect for leakage whenever possible. The pipeline made abrupt turns at nearly right angles so that its route could conform to the Italian terrain, and followed along roads, dipped into valleys and carried up over hills. Additional booster pumping stations were necessary because of rugged terrain.
—*Photo by John T. Mason, 196th Signal Photo Company, February, 1945
111-SC-202904
(National Archives)*

HARRY B. MORGAN.

MRS. MARGUERITE MORGAN of 1323 Jefferson street, Charlotte, has been notified by the War department that her son, Technician Fourth Grade Harry B. Morgan, 25, photographer in the Signal corps of Lieut. Gen. Mark Clark's Fifth Army, died on November 16 of wounds which he received in action in Italy November 12. An earlier War department telegram had told of the wounds, and the message concerning his death arrived four days later.

In addition to his mother, Technician Morgan leaves his father, Russell B. Morgan of Washington; a sister, Mrs. Philip E. Bartlett of Route 1 Charlotte, and a grandmother, Mrs. Ella Clark of Wilmington. He was a graduate of Central High school, class of 1937, had worked, successively, at St. John's studio, and Dunbar's studio, and for a time had been employed in the mailing room of The Charlotte Observer. He enlisted in April, 1942, and went overseas on November, 1943.

Charlotte Observer
Dec. 5, 1944

Still photographer T/4 Harry B. Morgan, 25, died of wounds sustained on November 16, 1944 in a Luftwaffe bombing in the Italian village of Monghidoro which also claimed the life of fellow photographer Staff Sergeant Cecil Max Campbell in the same incident. Both men were assigned to the 3131st Signal Service Company. Morgan is buried at the U.S. Military cemetery south of Florence. Don Wiedenmayer and his wife Shirley visited his gravesite in 1971.

Used with permission of the Charlotte Observer

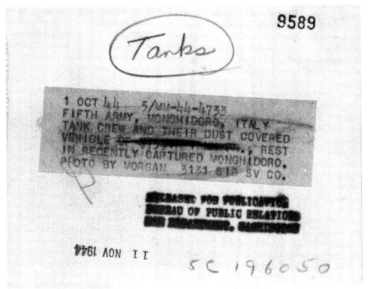

Tankers of the 752nd Tank Battalion rest in the recently captured village of Monghidoro, Italy. The photo was cleared for publication on November 11, 1944, the week Morgan lost his life in action.

5/MM-44-4733
Photo by Harry B. Morgan,
3131 Signal Service Company

Photographer Cecil Max Campbell, 3131st Signal Service Company is buried at the city of Mesa cemetery, Mesa, Arizona. Born on Nov. 15, 1921, he was killed in action in Italy on November 12, three days before his 23rd birthday. Campbell was killed in the same bombing attack which also claimed the life of fellow photographer Harry B. Morgan and wounded a third enlisted man. An American flag is placed beside his Arizona gravesite each Memorial Day and a special memorial service is given at the Mesa City Cemetery in honor of Campbell and all veterans buried there.

Photo courtesy of Mesa City Cemetery, Mesa, Arizona

Captured Germans march by their dead in Verona, Italy towards a prisoner of war compounded in late April 1945 guarded by an 88th Division infantry soldier. At the road junction of Route 62 and 12 in the city of Verona, Italy, Fifth Army soldiers of Co. E, 2nd Battalion, 351st Regiment of the 88th Division, and a tank destroyer of the 805th Tank Destroyers, Co. B, caught the Germans by surprise. John Mason was reassigned by the 196th SPC a new photo team at the start of the final spring offensive. He did not see his former partner, Burke O'Connell until the end of the war when all 196th SPC personal were recalled by company headquarters in Montecatini, Italy to prepare to return home.

—Photo by John T. Mason, 196th Signal Photo Company

An Army ambulance evacuates wounded from the front lines near Highway 65, between Loiano and Livergnano in this photo dated January 5, 1945. The flow of wounded from the battlefield was carefully controlled. Evacuation hospitals were kept as free of patients as possible, thereby affording immediate facilities for the most urgent cases.
Photo by John T. Mason, 3131st Signal Service Company

Burke O'Connell crouches in the snow holding his Bell and Howell Eyemo 35-mm motion picture camera in second of three photos along Highway 65, between the ruined villages of Loiano and Livergnano. The first snowfall of the season covered the higher mountains on November 11, 1944 and four days later two inches of snow and rain deluged the Apennines. The use of chains on Allied military vehicles, constant work by snowplows, and the almost never-ending hand labor by thousands of soldiers and civilians kept the roads open.
Photo by John T. Mason, 3131st Signal Service Company

An additional photo taken the same, cold, snowy day shows an Allied truck convoy along Highway 65 heading towards the front lines.

Photo by John T. Mason, 196th Signal Photo Company

The smoldering ruins of the town of Loiano, Italy along Highway 65 seen in late October 1944. Three regiments of the 91st Division including the 361st Infantry joined in the fight to clear determined German resistance. Loiano and nearby Mount Bastia fell to the 3rd Battalion, 362nd Infantry, on the afternoon of October 5th, 1944 but more than three days of tough fighting were required to wrest Mount Castellari, two miles to the north, from the fresh German 65th Grenadier Division.

—*Photo by Donald Wiedenmayer, 3131st Signal Service Company*

An undated, uncaptioned, Signal Corps negative from the author's wartime photo collection captures the mud, misery and gritty persistence of Allied combat forces as they steadily battered their way north through heavy German resistance towards the Alps.
(O'Connell collection)

Two oxen are guided along a snowy path by a helpful Italian partisan who aides in the evacuation of an American casualty on an improvised litter. Use of a three-letter code "OCO" and number "44" by the Army Pictorial Service in this undated photo identifies the print as having been taken by O'Connell in late 1944.
Photo by Burke O'Connell,
3131st Signal Service Company

Private Roy Humphrey is being given blood plasma by Pfc. Harvey White, after he was wounded by shrapnel, on August 9, 1943 in Santa Agata, Sicily. Publication of this photograph taken by Lt. John S. Wever, 196th Signal Photo Company, was widely used in supporting Red Cross blood drives during the war.
—*U.S. Army photo, National Archives, 111-SC-178198*

T/5 John Pitts, a motion picture cameraman with the Army Pictorial Service, uses a Bell and Howell 35-mm Eyemo motion picture camera to film the first South African tank to cross the Reno River on the way to Bologna.
Photo by 2d Lt. Robert Schmidt,
196th Signal Photo Company
111-SC-329873,
(National Archives)

An 88th Division infantry squad is seen being briefed by an officer in the Monterumici-Mount Adone ridge area of Italy in April 1945. The efforts of the entire 88th Division and part of the 91st Division during the drive to Bologna were directed towards taking the boot-shaped Monterumici-Mount Adone ridge from a well dug in enemy, the German 8th Mountain Division which was determined to hold.

Photo by 2d Lt. Robert Schmidt, 196th Signal Photo Company

Staff Sgt. Bernard Kreselewski of the 337th Field Artillery Battalion of the 88th Division, numbers a keg of gold prior to it being loaded onto a truck in the Fortezza area of Italy. Standing guard at the table is Pfc. Charles O'Cline, 349th Infantry Regiment, 88th Division, while 1st Lt. Carl O. Nordberg, 337th Field Artillery, 88th Division, checks the marking. Col. E. O. Howell, Senior Finance Officer, 5th Army, looks on.

Photo by 196th Signal Photo Company, dated May 17, 1945, National Archives

Chapter 20

"Heaven's to Hemorrhoids"

Free from duty while recovering from hemorrhoids, Burke is unexpectedly assigned to new duties outside of unit headquarters in Pistoia to process camera equipment. Orders to the 180th Signal Repair Detachment which will give him a few cherished weeks of personal freedom and offer hope to see his love, Tina Calamai, are a welcome answer to his prayers.

Verona, Italy, May 30, 1945

One thing my unfortunate medical condition did for me was to keep me from being assigned any work-related company duties.

Other photographers in my unit were now busy drawing unpleasant duties as KP, guard duty or whatever else our commanding officer might require of us.

John was then stuck on a work detail, along with my good friend, Staff Sgt. Dave Kurland, cleaning up piles of our still and motion picture camera equipment which had been recently turned in.

Until I was medically cleared fit for duty, I had little to do.

It was while I was doing just that one day when former First Sergeant, Walter R. Emrich, Jr., called me into his office. I'd known Emrich since we first served together in the 3131st Signal Service Company in Algiers. He had since received a field commission to second lieutenant and now served as our unit's personnel officer.

He politely asked about my delicate condition, and even though I could say at that moment I was feeling much better, I was still listed on the no duty list and I was going to see that my name remained there for as long as I could.

Emrich was, for all intents and purposes, a nice guy in the 196th's unit personnel office. Having always been away from the company, I never got to know him very well but all reports about him from my peers in the unit were always favorable.

"Burke, I know you can't handle any detail work but I've got something that I think would be just fine for you," he said, as he shuffled through some papers.

"The job I have in mind for you would keep you away from headquarters."

I told him that whatever he had in mind would be well worth hearing. I considered Emrich to be a fair guy, and I knew he wouldn't throw me any fast balls that I couldn't catch.

"We've got to send all our photographic and lab equipment to an Army quartermaster packing and crating depot where it will all be boxed according to the space required for shipment to the United States. They want us to send a detail to oversee and supervise the packing. I'd like you to be on that detail."

I began to get excited about this thing and felt that somewhere along the line my heavenly "protectors" had been working overtime.

"Where is this depot located?"

"Well, it happens to be a place I think you know well. It's in Pistoia."

"Pistoia, sir, you've got to be kidding," I heard myself saying.

I could only think of the 20 kilometers that separated Pistoia from Colli Alti where the Villa Calamai was located.

"No, I'm not kidding. Why should I be?"

"Well, you know, just as a manner of speaking. Sure. It sounds great. When do I leave?"

"Maybe tomorrow; I will let you know."

"Say, sir, could John Mason be on that detail?"

Emrich shook his head.

"No, I'm afraid not. The C.O. has him on his own special detail."

I turned to leave just as the lieutenant interrupted me.

"Another thing, Sergeant. The unit will be leaving Verona to go to Montecatini staging area for embarkation to the United States. So there is no need for you to come back here to Verona."

He revealed that our unit's likely staging area was to be Montecatini Val di Cecina, located south of Verona, in the province of Pisa.

"If there's anything you want to know about, I will tell you. So you can drag out the detail as long as you want. Take good care of yourself. You don't want to go back to the States with hemorrhoids, do you?"

"Not if I can help it. Thanks, sir, it was especially nice of you to think of me. I really appreciate it, more than I can say."

When I left his office, I was literally walking on air!

My hemorrhoids had fast become a thing of the past.

Chapter 21

A reunion with Tina

Pistoia, Italy, May 30, 1945

I received orders on May 30, 1945 to proceed as part of an advance party to the 180th Signal Repair Detachment for the purpose of processing equipment.

First Lieutenant Edward R. Ager led the eight man detachment which was to last nearly a month and also included my former partner, still photographer Don Wiedenmayer.

We worked in a large warehouse factory building in Pistoia which had been used to crate glass wine flasks and large demijohns for the glass works at nearby Empoli.

Our convoy had brought a considerable amount of our own photographic equipment for repair and processing, and there would be several truck loads of gear coming down later from Montecatini to keep us busy.

Fellow photographers Jack Rubin and Pete Yaskell, both of whom I had shared the road from Rome, were also assigned to the detail. Pfc. Adolph J. Pollock served as one of the 2-1/2 ton truck drivers.

The process of our detailed inspection and unpacking of the camera gear went slow.

Pete Yaskell enjoyed handling every still and motion picture camera that we had to pack, and in a way, you had to admire his thoroughness and professionalism. At times he couldn't pick up one still camera without pressing each and every shutter release button he touched.

I was delighted to discover I could sign out an Army jeep for personal use when my daily duties had ended and then delightedly drove off alone towards the Villa Calamai at the very first opportunity I was given.

"Oh, bless your hemorrhoids!" Tina exclaimed when I saw her and told her the whole story.

"Burke, I just can't believe it."

Our good friend, Rina, who had been practicing her English throughout the winter sadly said, "Why no John have no hemorrhoids, no like you?"

"Maybe John will develop some later, but he's coming to see you, Rina just as soon as he can."

"John will be in Montecatini soon and I'll get him over here some way."

It was amazing that I could still be in the U.S. Army and be so completely free again. Of course, the situation was not going to last forever but while it did, I was going to treasure each and every wonderful moment of it.

I took a moment to gratefully thank my lucky stars, or my 'protectors,' or whomever, for showering on me such a blessing.

It was like being on "Civvy Street," out of uniform with no military responsibilities whatsoever at long last.

I worked at the camera processing facility in Pistoia each day until about 4:00 o'clock p.m. when I could leave with the jeep for the villa each evening. I only had to return to Pistoia at 7 a.m. just in time for breakfast roll call.

As I made the early morning drive back to Pistoia, feeling the fresh cool air of the country in my face, I thought of how my entire relationship with Tina had been built on a series of coincidences.

Everything had dovetailed as though it had been planned, so I guess coincidence should not be an accurate term to describe what continued to bring us together.

Events kept falling steadily into place like pieces of a jigsaw puzzle with such uncanny accuracy that made me really wonder, and at times, afraid of what was to come.

Was fate steadily leading each of us towards something?

Was Tina simply tempting me with poison apples, so I would end up a victim of my own choice?

We enjoyed the moments Tina and I could now spend together while I was assigned to Pistoia, and I was delighted to learn from her a special letter had at last arrived.

Tina proudly told me upon my arrival one evening, "Today I have received a letter from someone in Riva di Garda."

"What did the letter say?"

The letter I sent her finally did get delivered at long last. I guessed that local mail delivery meant a return to normalcy in post-war Italy.

"Simply, he loves you, and that he misses you," I modestly told her.

"Yes, and he wrote, that no matter what happens to us, he will always find a way to come back to me."

"Do you believe that?" She shook her head.

"Okay then, I will tell you something. In today's *Stars and Stripes* newspaper, it says that Pan American Airways will start regular flights to Rome in a few days. That means that it's no longer the big problem to come here like it was before the war. You see, I could come back, zip, just like that."

She looked at me sadly.

I could read her thoughts.

"To come back, one has to leave first. After that, many things could complicate that "zip, just like that."

"Let's don't talk about that now. You're still here, so let's don't talk about you coming back. I will tell you what we will talk about. You said that this Sunday you are free all day. Why don't we take the bicycles and go to Florence?"

"Just how far is it?"

"It's about 12 kilometers. Rina and I have made that trip many, many times. And you are a young and strong American soldier." It was something that she had used many times when she needed something moved or lifted.

"Okay, I'm young and I'm strong, but remember, Sunday is my day of rest."

"Ufa, my love, you have rested all week."

Chapter 22

Tales of the "Blue Cat"

Florence, Italy, June, 1945

Florence had been especially beautiful when I first saw it in the summer of 1944 and the difference a year had made was remarkable.

Tina's good friend Rina, Tina and I now leisurely pedaled our bicycles through the city where almost a year before John and I had accompanied a combat scouting patrol of the British Army across the Arno River into the city while under frequent enemy fire.

The Sunday morning the three of us arrived in Florence, we found the city streets again crowded with people on bicycles urgently heading to and from their destinations. We noticed as we traveled along the winding banks of the Arno River as it weaved through central Florence that while reconstruction had already begun, the ugly skeletal reminders of the recent war were still visible in the ruins of proud, centuries-old historic bridges and buildings reduced to ruins by the retreating German armies.

Even our own Allied military vehicular traffic was obscured by the sheer density of the Florentine people now out enjoying every cherished moment of glorious 1945 summer sun.

We rode over to the Arno and then hand carried our bicycles across the shallow river bottom which had become the primary manner to get across from one side to the other. We then pedaled our bicycles along the beautiful, tree-lined Viale dei Colli towards the Piazza Michelangelo. Piazza Michelangelo sits on a hill on the south bank of the Arno River, just east of the center of Florence. Designed in 1869 by Poggi, the plaza offers a great view of the city, and is still a very popular contemporary tourist destination.

We sat at an outside table of a restaurant in the piazza with a panoramic view hard to equal anywhere else in the world now before us as we enjoyed our cake and ice cream.

How was it possible to be enjoying such a moment, when not all that long ago, the Allied armies had just locked up hundreds of thousands of German prisoners of war in compounds only a hundred miles north?

The situation was such a paradox.

I had lived so long in the dirt and grime of the war that to now find myself clean wearing a freshly pressed uniform sitting there handsomely with Tina and Rina and now eating the gods' own nectar of desserts and drinking Vin Santo, made me feel like I never really knew the side of myself that had roamed the dusty by-roads of Italy, taking pictures of the ugliness of war.

The European war was now officially over, but there on that single summer day, it was as though the war had never happened to anyone at all.

Tina's birthday in July was coming soon, and I drove into the city of Florence alone thinking of gifts I might buy for her. I discovered what may have been one of the very few bottles of her favorite Guerlain Parisian perfume then available for sale in Florence and made it one of my first purchases.

The beautifully sculpted glass bottle was an exquisite work of art, one I was certain Tina would always treasure.

A fellow photographer in my unit, Kelly Litt, told me of a rather unique ornamental ceramics factory named Zaccagnini which he recommended that I should see.

With some difficulty, I found the factory he described and introduced myself to the owner, a pleasant, comic-opera type who had a thick, heavy moustache.

I explained to him that I wanted to buy a very special ceramic cat for a personal gift.

"You have come to the right place. I want you to know, I am the holder of the Disney reproductions license for Italy. Cats, dogs, mice—I've got them all. You all know that Mickey Mouse has friends. I have them here. Come, I show you."

Zaccagnini guided me through his factory that had been reduced to a modest workforce of just himself and a few young boys as his assistants.

He was right. The factory was full of fabulous and readily familiar ceramic cartoon animals.

Signore Zaccagnini crafted all sorts of ceramic art and ceramic castings of the popular Disney characters of the day which in Italy were still very much in demand.

"Signore Zaccagnini," I told him, "What I want to buy is a large cat."

Before I could finish explaining to him, he pulled me over to a shelf.

"Do you like this one?

I forget his name, but he is the biggest cat I have."

The cat he showed me was about 12 inches long. His front paws and chin were almost touching the ground while his hind legs and tail stood up straight. He was in a kind of crawling, crouching position. This cat was exactly the one I wanted, but I had a very different color in mind.

"OK, that's fine. But he has to be blue. This one is brown. I want mine blue."

Tina had affectionately nicknamed me her "Gatto Bleu" or blue cat, and I would accept no color than what I wanted.

"It's not possible, Signore Sargente.

Mr. Disney wants this cat to be brown, and brown he has to be. I am the holder of the Disney..." he stammered.

"Yeah, I know, you told me. But my cat has to be blue.

I don't give a damn for Walt Disney."

He still vigorously protested. I could tell Signore Zaccagnini was very serious about Mr. Disney.

"How much is this cat?" I asked him.

"This cat costs eight hundred lira."

His price was the equivalent of about eight U.S. dollars.

"I'll tell you what. You make this gatto blue for me and I will pay you twelve hundred lira. But this cat has to be blue."

"Okay, but you know, I'm supposed to sell these cats only in brown. But for you, I'll make him blue. You mustn't tell anyone."

I raised my right hand and swore I wouldn't disclose our little secret.

I returned to the ceramics factory two days later and picked up my cat which was glazed a beautiful shade of sky blue.

Even the owner Zaccagnini himself had to admit that this ceramic cat for me now looked better in blue than it did in its original brown.

Chapter 23

Axis Sally leaves the airwaves

One morning as I was driving my jeep back to Pistoia from the Villa Calamai, an unexpected event happened to me that seemed to close a circle that began when I first reported overseas for duty in Tunisia.

It was about 7:00 a.m. when I passed by a cluster of stone buildings just inside Pistoia that I saw a jeep with its side curtains up parked diagonally in the street, blocking my way.

I noticed a weary sergeant who stood in front of his jeep opposite me and as I came closer towards him, he discretely waved his hands in an attempt to draw my attention. I could see that he wore an Army Counter Intelligence Corps (CIC) arm band on the sleeve of his field jacket.

I quickly parked my jeep and swiftly walked over towards him.

I could tell he was in a very tired state with more than a few days' beard, but I always knew CIC guys I had met tended to overplay their situation for dramatic effect.

His first words to me were clearly words I didn't want to hear at that moment.

"I've got to take your jeep."

I saw he was actually supporting himself on the hood of his jeep.

I naturally asked him the obvious question: "What's wrong with the one you have?"

"I've been driving all night south from Northern Italy. I guess I went to sleep and hit that highway marker. I must have broken something because the wheels are locked."

He introduced himself to me, and in a low, spy-like voice, said, "I have a very important prisoner in there." He motioned towards his jeep.

I looked over his shoulder but with the window curtains still up in his jeep, I still could not see much of anything.

He then quietly took me by the arm to give me a closer look.

"Did you ever hear of Axis Sally?"

I thought to myself, 'Is the Vatican in Rome?' Of course, I had heard of her. I was in North Africa when Allied soldiers gave her that nickname.

Just then, as though she had been called, a small, non-descript Italian woman in her late twenties stepped out of the jeep. Her clothes were rumpled and cheap-looking and her tousled black hair looked as though a comb hadn't been through it in weeks.

I could only imagine her serving up pizzas in a Ninth Avenue joint in New York. She was certainly not the glamour-voiced disc jockey of the German Afrika Korps I had heard.

Once out of the jeep, and in clear view, I said, "So, you're the gal we listened to in Tunisia."

She smiled modestly and shielded her eyes from the morning Italian sun.

I could sense this woman was more than a little embarrassed.

"Yes, I guess I am the one. Did you like my shows?" she said.

"Sure I did. But do you really want to know why all the GI soldiers kept you tuned in? Oh sure, the voice in the night turned a lot of them on. But the real truth was, you had such fantastic records. Our own armed forces radio didn't have such a library. How did you get such numbers?"

"I never really liked the Germans. Maybe at first, but later on, no. But I can tell you they had connections in New York and could get anything they wanted. You know, sometimes I would play a Glenn Miller record one month after it was released."

It was like I was hearing it again; the big band sounds, all the popular hits that every GI in his foxhole could relate to because he left a girl back there; the remembrance of the last dances at the USO.

Axis Sally became a route to nostalgia. It was like other generations found smoking grass, lying there in the dirt and thinking about all those wonderful nights that had gone before.

But she wasn't conning anyone with her propaganda.

No one threw their rifle and shouted that they wanted to go home. No, most soldiers just said over and over again, "Play it again, Sally."

I wondered if this Sally was the famous "Axis Sally," or just another in the group of English-speaking women used by the Germans to broadcast propaganda. I never did find out.

"What's your real name?" I asked her.

"It's Zucca. My father has a restaurant on 48th Street in New York, that is."

"Oh, sure, I know it well. My uncle's office is in the Playhouse Theatre just down the street."

Meanwhile, my friend the CIC seemed to be getting impatient with me.

"Well, what about giving me your jeep? I've got orders to get her to Florence."

I had grown attached to my jeep and didn't want to have to complete the rest of my journey on foot.

"Now you know I just can't give you a jeep. Not when it's signed out to me. I can't even take you to Florence because I've got to get to Pistoia.

The best thing is to flag down some Italian, if one comes along. If not, I'll go to Pistoia first, and then come back and take you."

An old gypsy-looking woman dressed in black with a shawl wrapped carefully walked out towards where we had gathered and slowly walked towards us. I saw that she was carefully holding something in her arms.

"Signora," she said, "che fa, che fa?"

The Zucca woman was a mother after all, and took the bundle bearing the baby from the old woman's arms.

She acknowledged the older woman in Italian and turned to us.

"This is my baby."

I looked down into the bundle of blankets. The little pink face rolled from side to side. She was obviously very happy to have the baby once again safely held in her young arms.

I could only think of the unhappiness that was in store for her.

Giving aid and comfort to the enemy, collaborationist or whatever they would hang on her was not going to make her future simple, not for her, nor for the baby. But then, I thought, who knows?

We are great and tough while we are winning, but once we have won, we become soft.

Finally, an Italian truck came along and stopped. The CIC was telling him something in Italian. But the driver was not understanding very much of it.

I wondered how a CIC guy could be an intelligence agent in Italy and speak such lousy Italian. But soon the pair got into the truck and left.

I watched the two of them drive down the road before me, thinking for this "Axis Sally" what was now an ignominious end to what had been previously such an illustrious career, but then, who knows?

Maybe I'll hear that voice again after the war over some late night station in New York, still playing all the old big-band records for the drunks in some local city bars.

Time would tell.

Chapter 24

Return to Florence

Florence, June 1945

Sometime before, I had thrown out an off the cuff suggestion to Tina's father, Signore Raffaello that he write a letter to the Allied Military Government for Occupied Territories (AMG) headquarters concerning the loss of his cattle which had been taken from his family during the German occupation.

The Allies established military rule within Italy during the Second World War in the territory they occupied. Claims for lost property could be submitted to the AMG for consideration.

It seemed that the older gentleman took my advice and actually wrote them. I was surprised to learn he actually received an answer to his claim in such a short time and that the AMG's answer to him would be a most affirmative decision.

A special agricultural section had been established to deal with herds of stray cattle which had been picked up throughout Italy and were now to be redistributed, in proportions, to the Italian farmers who had lost them.

The official letter written to Signore Raffaello by the AMG directed him to go to the Piazza della Signoria, an L-shaped square in front of the Palazzo Vecchio in Florence to file his papers.

The only problem Tina's father now faced in getting to Florence was that I was prohibited to carry civilians as passengers in my Army jeep.

I learned of a local family in the village of Colli Alti that still owned a pre-war four-door Fiat 500 which still worked but didn't have any fuel. The family had managed to keep their family car safe from being confiscated by the Germans by hiding it deep in a barn covered with straw.

I knew Tina's family had been forced to surrender both of their family automobiles during the German occupation. I told Tina's father, Signore Raffaello, to tell the owner of the Fiat I would gladly fill up the fuel tank of their automobile, if the local family would be generous enough to allow me to use it for transportation to Florence when I needed it.

We soon made a deal, and before long, Tina and I were able to drive her father to the right office in downtown Florence to file his claim. While he was busily handling his affairs, which we knew meant sweating out waiting in an endless line, Tina and I drove around the city sightseeing.

Our use of a private, family automobile meant that for once as a driver, I was outside the immediate jurisdiction and authority of the local Allied military police. Its use kept Tina from receiving the ridicule many Florentines dubbed attractive, Italian women who rode in the front passenger seats of either American or Allied jeeps, which was "jeepista." That was the last thing I ever wanted Tina to be called.

We parked the Fiat and began walking down Via di Tornabuoni towards the Arno River. Tina stopped in front of a small stone Catholic church she recognized in the small piazza.

"This is the Catholic church where I was married. It's very beautiful inside," she said.

"Let's go in," I replied. "I always find churches rather cool and comfortable."

Tina and I went into the darkened stillness of the small but very decorative church. We saw a few people kneeling in prayer saying their rosaries and others seated quietly in reflection.

Tina gently took my hand as we stood near the main altar. I felt it tighten around my fingers. Somewhere in my mind came the wish that someone, somewhere, would make all this that was between us, really happen. Make it all come true and not remain just a wartime romance with the obvious ending. That somehow it would all come together.

When we walked out of the church, I was looking up at a familiar statue.

"Tina, I took a photograph of that same sculpture when John and I first came through the city of Florence on that patrol, the first time in Florence.

It seems like a long time ago. I believe I called it, 'blind justice.'"

The statue of "lady justice" ranks as one of the most well known statues in the world and traces its origins from ancient Greek and Roman times.

The lady represented is Themis, the goddess of justice and law. Well known for her clear sightedness, she typically holds a sword in one hand and scales in the other.

Tina looked up at it and said, "There's a funny story about it."

Interested in hearing more, I replied, "We'll go up to Doney's Tea Room at the Excelsior Hotel you spoke of earlier.

We'll have some pastries and you can tell me all about it. I love stories."

Doney's was well known throughout the 1930s among Florentines as a favorite intimate setting in the Excelsior Hotel for light lunches, drinks or the exclusive Sunday brunch.

Tina began to tell me the story of a very strange bird.

An old Italian marchesa, a noblewoman had lived in an apartment across from the church where she was married. Her husband was an Italian army colonel who served in Mussolini's invasion of Ethiopia and had brought back with him a very strange bird.

The bird was quite large in size, and resembled a crow, with a long yellow beak.

One day the marchesa found a favorite rhinestone bracelet missing.

She had just recently hired a new young maid and she naturally cast her suspicions on her, since only a girl from the country would be fooled by taking a rhinestone bracelet.

She questioned the girl without success. Later on, she discovered a ring with many small diamonds missing. She again began to have very real suspicions about her young maid's honesty.

The marchesa discovered the bird would often make strange noises like it was trying to talk. Then, after a time, she discovered another necklace missing.

Tina said the marchesa had little choice then but to fire the girl, which she did.

Before the girl left, the marchesa had left her jewelry box open on the dresser in her room. When she came back from accompanying the girl to her front door, she returned to discover her jewelry box was empty.

The marchesa felt that the matter was now a case for the police and called upon a good friend in the Carabinieri who had served with her husband to help.

There was little the police officer could do but to catch the girl and make her confess. As they were talking, the bird flitted from one piece of furniture inside the home to another and then to the open window sill.

The policeman then asked about the unusual looking bird. He had also seen this same type of bird before in Ethiopia and asked the Marchesa if she had a very large, sparkling ring he could borrow for a moment.

She obliged him by taking one from her finger. The policeman laid the ring on the table and then escorted the Marchesa out of the room, closing the door behind them and leaving the bird alone in the room.

They went into the other room and watched from an adjacent window. What they saw would have made the fictional French gentleman thief, Arsene Lupin hang his head in shame. Lupin appears in a book series of detective fiction / crime fiction novels written by French writer Maurice Leblanc, a contemporary of Arthur Conan Doyle, famously known for his stories about the detective Sherlock Holmes.

The large, funny bird sailed out the window and with the large ring safely in its beak, flew right up to the sculpture which featured the uplifted scales of justice and gently deposited the ring in the round plate.

"Now, Marchesa," the policeman said to her triumphantly, "all we need is the fire department. I am sure you will find all your other jewelry in the same place."

Sure enough, this strange Ethiopian bird, earned its nickname that day of "la gazza ladra" (*The Thieving Magpie*) from the opera by Gioacchino Rossini written in 1817 of the same name which featured a similar character.

The sculpture's round plate contained all of the bird's spoils, nested there neatly and safely atop the little piazza at the end of Via Tornabuoni.

People might wonder why this particular bird chose, of all places, the scales of justice to hide its ill-gotten goods. Maybe this bird had the same ironic sense of humor and respect for authority most pigeons have when they perch majestically atop the spike of the helmet of a beloved general of some past war and leave their droppings behind.

A water-damaged photo shows civilians crossing the Reno River by bicycle, north of Bologna, Italy. April 1945. Donald Wiedenmayer recalls climbing out of his jeep he shared with Burke to retrieve his own 35mm camera case and other camera equipment from being swept down river when their jeep unexpectedly stalled and sank in rising water. The two photographers and their driver, James Morris sought to use their jeep to carry a young mother and her baby across the river to safety. O'Connell led the woman and child to shore while a nearby weapons carrier used a tow cable to pull Don and Jim out of the drink.

Photo by Donald Wiedenmayer, 196th Signal Photo Company

The end of the Italian campaign is celebrated by soldiers from the 44th Division and the 10th Mountain Division at the Italo-Austrian border. Photographer Donald Wiedenmayer was there to capture the joyous celebration and delighted to learn that his photo made the May 11, 1945 front page Stars and Stripes Mediterranean.

Used with permission from the Stars and Stripes. © 1945, 2006 Stars and Stripes

Enthusiastic infantrymen of 34th Infantry Regiment, 44th Division, Seventh Army on far side rush towards a border crossing in early May 1945 at Resia Pass, between Italy and Austria to greet soldiers of the Fifth Army, 10th Mountain Division, 86th Regiment, on the near side.

Photo by Donald Wiedenmayer, 196th Signal Photo Company

Burke O'Connell, left center of the photograph holds his Bell and Howell newsreel camera while filming soldiers of the 752nd Tank Battalion at the Italian-Swiss border at Munster, Switzerland.

Photo by Donald Wiedenmayer, 196th Signal Photo Company

Lieutenant Herb Mahn explains to a curious Swiss border guard the operations of a hand-held microphone used to communicate with crewmen inside. Wiedenmayer recalled climbing onto the tank and later submitting the photo for consideration to Fifth Army headquarters. Mahn has a framed print on display in his Connecticut home ever since the war and was delighted to learn the photographer, Donald Wiedenmayer of the 196th Signal Photo Company was the one who captured the moment for history.

Photo by Donald Wiedenmayer, 196th Signal Photo Company

Burke talks to a Swiss border guard at the Munster, Switzerland crossing. This casual photo led to the discovery of another Signal Corps photo taken by Don Wiedenmayer of the same Swiss guard climbing up onto a tank of the 752nd Tank Battalion to talk to its commander, 1st Lt. Herb Mann.

Photo by Donald Wiedenmayer, 196th Signal Photo Company

Photographer Don Wiedenmayer, 28, sits on the Italian-Swiss border gate at Munster, Switzerland, May 1945.

Photo by Burke O'Connell, 196th Signal Photo Company

German prisoners were often wide-eyed at the sight of being guarded by Japanese-American soldiers at the Fifth Army Enemy Concentration Area in Brescia, Italy. Here, Pfc. Genso Tocuchi, Headquarters Company, 100th Battalion, 442nd Infantry Regiment of Honolulu, Hawaii and Sgt. Seisaburo, Headquarters Company, 100th Battalion, 442nd Infantry Regiment, also of Honolulu, Hawaii, inspect a horse-drawn German field kitchen. Photographers of the 196th Signal Photo Company including Wiedenmayer and O'Connell documented daily life of his sprawling post-war prisoner of war compound.
Army Signal Corps Photo, 18 May 1945
5/MM-45-9817

U.S. Fifth Army Concentration Area, Ghedi Airfield, Brescia, Italy. German Motor Pool, 14th German Army. Hundreds of camouflaged German military vehicles, ambulances and automobiles of all types filled the surrounding airfield at Ghedi. Tens of thousands of surrendering Germans were held at the facility at the end of the war.
(O'Connell collection)

Fifth Army photographers, Martin G. Brooks, left and Sam Spirito, right, of the 196th Signal Photo Co. tour Venice, Italy in a gondola in an official U.S. Army photo dated May 1, 1945. Don describes the scene. "Upon arrival in Venice we were stopped by the British Red Caps (military police). When they saw our passes said *"By Command of Field Marshal Alexander"* they couldn't get us on our way any faster. We lunched at the Ristorante Cavaletto just off the Piazzo San Marco in the company of British officers." A second close-up color photograph taken that same day also taken by Wiedenmayer captures Burke, center, with Martin Brooks at left, Burke O'Connell and Sam Spirito, right.

Photos by Donald Wiedenmayer, 196th Signal Photo Company, May 1, 1945

Burke shakes hands with Corporal Weintraub of the 163rd Signal Photo Company at Resia Pass across the Italian-Austrian border.

"After the American tanks had taken up positions along the road and the squads of infantrymen were deployed, Don and I noticed across the border some infantry soldiers steadily coming our way," O'Connell recalled.

"One of them enthusiastically started running toward me. I saw he was carrying what appeared to be a Speed Graphic still camera." "My God, I thought, he's an Army photographer."

The U.S. Seventh Army marched all across Europe and there in the little town of Nauders in Austria, had finally linked up with the one who had started the whole fight in Italy three years before, General Mark Clark's small but courageous, Fifth Army.

—*Photo by Donald Wiedenmayer, 196th Signal Photo Company*

Chapter 25

A summer picnic to remember

Villa Calamai, Colli Alti, June, 1945

John and I returned to the Villa Calamai with a noticeable personal feeling of accomplishment. Apparently officials of the Allied Military Government in Florence were willing to recognize the loss of Tina's father, Signore Raffaello's livestock and he would be compensated with a replacement herd of cattle for his loss.

It had been a beautiful day for Tina and I. Florence seemed like a different city. Being with someone you love will make any city seem exciting and different.

We visited all of our favorite places in Florence which held special memories for us including those where tourists frequently visited before the war began. Tina had also taken time to share with me many of the out-of-the way places within the city not seen on the usual tourist routes.

It had been a day of joy and satisfaction. Little did I know that it was to have been my last.

As we were waiting for dinner, we heard a commotion from Beppa and Lucia in the kitchen. We went to investigate and found John standing in the doorway. He had come to the villa from nearby Montecatini by way of an Army supply truck. The driver had dropped him off in Colli Alti and he walked up to the main entrance of the villa.

The typical scene of past arrivals at the Villa Calamai by John and I always seemed to be memorable. Family dogs could usually be seen barking and running around and Tina's extended family members Beppa and Lucia always greeted us full of joy. Her father, old Signore Raffaello always seemed to be on hand to welcome us.

John's arrival brightened everyone's mood. While Tina, Rina and I did not speak of it too much, we felt a certain sadness about the villa with John. The evening of his arrival at the Villa Calamai felt like old times. The four of us were all together happily once more.

We each wondered to ourselves, for how much longer?

"The way I see it," John said, seated before the villa's fireplace, while holding a half-full wine glass, "there's not too much time for either of us."

"Pretty soon they're going to run out of things for headquarters to have us do at Montecatini, and then we will be quickly ordered on our way back to the States," I chimed in.

"What the hell are they trying to tell us anyway?"

I tried my best in my own way to lighten the mood of the situation.

"They're trying to get us sort of civilized before they turn us loose on the continent of the United States."

"You mean that they don't want us walking up to decent American girls smartly saying, "Dove, casa?"

"Something, like that."

John lit a cigarette.

"What I want to know is, what are you thinking about; you know, Tina?

I know it's going to be hell for you leaving her," he said sadly.

John added, "Christ, if I was free, I would probably feel the same way. But, you know what I mean."

John had been married before the war began.

I poured a little more cognac.

"John, I have been thinking this thing over for some time now. I honestly think I will be coming back over here, once I'm out of the Army."

"Come back over here? What the hell would you do? What would you come here for? Oh, I know how you feel about Tina," he continued, "but you've got to think about how it will be later.

Jesus, Burke, after all the GIs get out of here, things will return to normal and life will go just as though there had never been a war.

You would just become some leftover relic of the war, just like those burned-out tanks that are still on the road.

I don't mean to say that Tina's feelings for you would change. You have to ask yourself, what does she really want from you, and in turn, what do you honestly want from her?"

I didn't have an easy answer to John's blunt question.

"Burke, maybe we're seen as the big heroes; the ones at the head of the parade. Once we do get this damn uniform off, once and for all, you know you won't be able to tell us from any other two guys in the crowd. Maybe you should just let things ride for a while, and see how things work out for the both of you."

John reminded me that our unit's former signal photo officer, Colonel Melvin Gillette had received orders to move from the Italian campaign to the recently liberated Philippines in advance of the likely Allied invasion of the Japanese mainland later that summer.

"Remember, there's always Colonel Gillette waiting over in the Philippines."

It made me laugh when I thought of it. "You know what Tina said when I told her that I was going to get out of the Army and come back? She said, 'if they were going to let you out of the Army they would not have given you a new pair of shoes.' John, what I'm saying is what I feel. What I will be able to do is something else again."

"Let's see what happens. Hell, maybe I might even come back with you," John jokingly replied.

"Hey John, what about your wife? You're not going to leave her?"

His face became rather sullen. "Maybe she's leaving me. At least her last letter read like that. It has happened to a lot of guys who went overseas."

"Well then, why not come back with me? We'll open a photographic studio."

John raised his glass. "Whatever happens, just remember that we really had some good times together. It was great while it lasted."

"And it isn't over yet. There will still be some good times ahead. Let's drink to that." We both drained our glasses and went to dinner.

Chapter 26

A birthday date

196th SPC Headquarters, late June, 1945

Tina's upcoming July birthday couldn't have come any too soon for me.

As I had been expecting for a while, we received our orders to finish up cleaning and turning in our camera equipment in the village, Pistoia and to join the remaining troops of the unit in Montecatini.

The official packing job had already been finished for several days, but those of us assigned to this detachment creatively delayed our departure for as long as we could until making our two-hour drive.

Within days of our arrival in Montecatini on June 1, 1945, and after we reported in after our two-hour drive, we were pushed into attending a series of movies, sex lectures and the principles of the Japanese language which I had no desire to ever putting to practical use.

We had the usual inoculation shots and medical examinations to make us either fit or unfit to enter the United States. The Army paymasters brought all of our individual pay records up to date and I was paid in full for the first time in three years. But then, where I had spent most of my time, money wasn't too much of a necessity.

The company was really good about giving us leave. They ran two trucks every evening to Florence with a return trip about midnight. Since the road the Army trucks took passed the Signa intersection which was only about a half mile from the villa, it made it very convenient for John and I to return to the Villa Calamai almost every night. This was a considerable stroke of luck on our part and made our presence at Tina's upcoming birthday party a sure thing.

Having lived a alone a lot and away from the family, birthdays had almost always gone by with little or no fanfare. Sometimes they were completely forgotten. So it was a real treat to be at Tina's birthday celebration.

The Italians really go all out for such important personal occasions. There was no end to the amount of food and the quality. It seemed that everyone had worked for days preparing all the homemade pasta, cakes, special stuffed capon in gelatin and an endless amount of other dishes that turned the whole dinner into at least a 10-course meal. Signore Raffaello's private wine stock suffered quite a lot that night.

Tina liked the bottle of Jickey but what really grabbed her was the slouching, prowling blue cat. It was just something that she had never thought of and it delighted her so to know that I would go to the trouble to have something like that made up for her.

"You see, when I'm not here," I told her, "the blue cat will be prowling around on the lookout for you. He will protect you." This was about as easy a way to get into what I really had to tell her as I could think of.

"Tina, we won't be in Montecatini long. The Army is going to move us to another place," I solemnly said.

"Oh Dio, when? How long before you will leave?"

Her eyes searched mine for more details.

"Well, we will go to a place near Pisa, on the sea. We will then stay there until our transport ship is in the Leghorn harbor and then after it's there, we will board it."

The expression on her face grew steadily somber.

"Where near Pisa? How long will you be there?"

"It's near a place called Marina di Pisa. We will probably be there for maybe two or three days. It doesn't really matter."

Her face took on a curious expression of excitement. "Do you know that Rina has an aunt in Marina di Pisa? We have been thinking to go there to spend some time on the beach. If you're going to be there, we could come now."

"Wait a minute. That's in Pisa. How do you think you're going to get there? There aren't any buses, you know."

I began to get the feeling that arguing with Tina wasn't going to get me anywhere.

"We can come on bicycles."

"On bicycles, you've got to be crazy, that's at least 60 kilometers."

"It's really 85, but that doesn't make any difference. We are used to riding long distances. Maybe not that far, but it won't bother us."

"Look Tina, I know what you are saying and I would be a complete idiot not to feel happy about it but I just don't want you doing it. I would be afraid something might happen to the two of you. You know, this is a bad time of the war. Everyone is on the take for anything they can get. I wouldn't want you risking that. Hell, I don't know how long for sure we will be there. We might be gone before you get there."

Before the discussion could get any farther, John and Rina came in from the garden. Apparently, John had told Rina about where we would be going because as soon as she came into the room, she said, "Tina, they go to Marina di Pisa. I have told to John, I have an aunt there."

"Look John," I broke in, "do you know what these two women are trying to conjure up? They're going to travel on bicycles to Marina di Pisa to stay with Rina's aunt. On bicycles, that's 85 kilometers."

John looked surprised. "On bicycles, that's a lot of pedaling, kids. I don't think you should do it. It might even be dangerous."

I said quickly, "That's what I told Tina. You never know who you might meet on these roads."

Tina took me by the arm. "I want to spend as much time with you as I can. If this will give me a few more hours with you, then I want to do it. Don't you want that too?"

"Honey, we're talking about two different things. Of course I want to be with you as long as I can. But I don't want you to be risking something that could harm you very much. That Marina place will be so overrun with American soldiers and prostitutes and black marketers it won't be funny. You can imagine how these jumping off places are. You've heard how Naples was. Well, this won't be any different. It's just too big a chance to take; we may not even be there long or not be able to get out."

The look she gave me told me that her mind was made up. "It's a chance we are willing to take." She turned quickly to Rina and repeated it in Italian. Rina quickly agreed. "So you see, my dear blue cat, we will meet you there."

"Rina and I will meet you there."

"Where is there?" I asked.

"Burke, today is June 10th. You say you will probably not leave Montecatini for the next two days. That would be June 12th.

We can meet you on the steps of the Baptistery in the Piazza of the Leaning Tower of Pisa on June 14th. How does that sound?"

Rina quickly added, "Yes, how's that?"

John shrugged his broad shoulders. "What can we say?"

"Alright then," I said. "I can see there is no use in arguing with you, so we have a date then." I put my arms around Tina and looked deeply into her eyes. "What if we don't make it? What if we don't meet at the Baptistery? What then?"

"Then Gatto, this will be our goodbye, tonight. But I know we will meet. I just know it."

"I can't tell you how much I hope you are right," I said, trying to feel as confident as Tina.

We went out into the garden. When two people love each other, there are never too many fond farewell kisses. We kissed passionately, both believing, I think, that these farewell kisses could also be our last.

Chapter 27

Angels working overtime

Pisa, Italy 1945

Marina di Pisa is a modest seacoast village on the left of the Arno River where, after its twisting and turning, crawls through the central Tuscan country, finally lays itself out into the Tirranian Sea.

The area of Marina di Pisa was also on the border of what was probably the most notorious sectors of the Italian campaign.

Every part of the world where the war had touched had its lawless areas where just about everything and anything was the order of the day.

Not one of them could ever compare to the vicious and brutal reality that could be found in the city of Tombolo.

Between the cities of Livorno and Pisa, along the coastal beach area, there is a wide and dense forest which was formerly owned by King Victor Emmanuel.

Tall Roman pines had grown so close together that their umbrella tops touched one another to form a canopy. A dense undergrowth of dark vines and tall grassy weeds had formed together to make the area almost impenetrable.

The forest was about seven miles in depth and offered anyone seeking clandestine refuge a venerable, real equivalent of Robin Hood's "Sherwood Forest."

German army deserters were the first to take up residence in the forest, followed by Italian black marketers and local prostitutes. Some Italian partisans who turned from their participation in the war to the more lucrative career of bandits mingled easily with a steadily growing criminal element.

Some Allied soldiers found easy local contacts to sell stolen government property too easy to resist, and then fearing possible military court-martials for their crimes decided to go underground there.

Cheap prostitution was also available through a system of posted armed sentries who introduced the client into the heart of the forest. Nearly any sort of business could be safely transacted.

Prices were high and there were always waiting buyers for anything from cases of stolen cigarettes, whiskey, on up to the heavy stuff, which consisted of trailer loads of gasoline, stolen jeeps, new tires, and most types of weapons and ammunition.

Regular shipments of contraband and stolen Allied military goods were made available to the nearby cities and towns in the area and as far away as Florence.

The black market's ruling "gentry" dictated the official "law and order" of the forest. Personal differences were swiftly settled by a shot through the head and a nearby shallow grave.

Nearby, Marina di Pisa was also filled with similarly unsavory characters actively searching for the next gullible homeward-bound American GI still willing to make a last purchase for a high price.

I had second thoughts for Tina and Rina's safety traveling through this area in coming to meet us in Marina di Pisa. I knew what to expect in a place like that and since there was a strong local curfew in effect at night, I had guessed not much could happen to them if they traveled during daylight hours.

The time of our meeting on the steps of the Baptistery could not have been more precise. The two women had made the trip successfully on their bicycles without incident, leaving very early in the morning, arriving at Rina's aunts' home in Marina di Pisa before dark. Their journey had been an athletic, tour de force, but both women were excellent bicycle riders. The road leading to Marina di Pisa was relatively easy and flat and did not seem to affect them in any way.

Tina and I walked the steps up to the famous Leaning Tower, which had only recently been opened to the public. We each went in, saw the church, and watched the Galileo lamp swing suspended from the ceiling.

We also studied the intricate artistry of the pulpit, which contains some of the greatest assembly of sculpture and art work seen in any one place in Italy.

As we walked through the Piazza dei Miracoli, I was reminded of the first time John and I had seen it. I thought of all the things that had happened since then and how now, at this time, could it be ending? I think Tina must have had the same thoughts as she took my hand and we walked in silence across the lush green grass.

We made a date to meet the next day at the little square in front of the aunt's house. We had decided that we would go swimming, the beach being only a short way from there. We felt there would not be any difficulty getting away from the camp. We had made it to Pisa by jumping on a food ration supply truck that was going that way. But going to Marina di Pisa was just getting across a little footbridge over the Arno River.

I put my arms around Tina and told her the trip seemed much too long a way to come to spend so few hours together. But she felt that they were worth any bike ride she could ever make.

Inside of me, there was a feeling of profound gratefulness in these few moments that remained. In a way, I guess it was Tina's way of making some personal contribution toward our romance and a kind of counterbalance for all the distances I had traveled to see her.

Whatever it was, it really didn't make too much difference. The fact was that we were still holding out and staying together. We were cherishing every single moment together that we honestly could.

Fortunately for us, the official rules of our camp made it easy for John and me to leave any time we wanted to so long as we reported in by 6:00 o'clock p.m. for the mess hall's evening meal. We would try to meet up with Tina and Rina at around 11:00 o'clock in the morning and then go to the beach to swim.

Marina di Pisa, in the early 1900s, had been a very fashionable beach resort for the well-to-do families of Tuscany. There were still remaining the stylish old houses of that period. But in the ensuing years, the sea had slowly eroded most of the beachfront in the central part of the city that once had extended quite far out into the sea.

The general area had been built up with gazebos and lush trellised terraces, to say nothing of boardwalk piers that offered late afternoon strollers a last glimpse of the warm, afternoon sun as it slowly melted over the horizon.

Huge rock boulders could be seen stacked up against the main street as a man-made breakwater, lest the sea tear out the last remaining sign of a beachfront that over time had been steadily washed away.

South of the city of Marina di Pisa, the beachfront was in better shape and it was there that the four of us would swim and sunbathe. The sea was generally so beautiful and calm; it more closely resembled glass than it did water.

John and I typically brought along with us a large can of pineapple juice or orange juice which Rina and Tina were just crazy for.

He would dig a deep hole in the soft wet sand and bury the can to chill the juice until we were ready to enjoy the freshly made sandwiches Tina and Rina brought along for our picnic lunch.

Two enlisted American combat engineers walked up to John while he was busy digging a hole to bury his can of juice and asked if we would move for but a few moments so they could sweep the area with their magnetic detection gear.

All four of us stepped out into the surf and let them work.

We didn't find their request of us especially unusual, since considerable amounts of unexploded German and Allied mines and other ordnance was still littered across Italy waiting to kill or maim the unsuspecting human victim who stepped on them.

We looked back towards the engineers from the water as they urgently dug up our can of pineapple juice as if they intended to steal it from us.

John yelled back at them.

"Hey guys, that's our juice. I put it there to get it cool."

One of the engineers was still on his knees excavating more of the sand surrounding the steel can with his hands.

"That can of pineapple juice may be yours, buddy," he yelled, "but this German mine buried right next to it sure as hell isn't!"

Just then the two engineers gingerly unearthed a buried still active German Teller mine not six inches away from the pineapple juice can that John buried.

The Teller mine was the standard anti-tank mine used by German forces during World War II. The mine exploded when its protruding pin was forced into the mine due to the pressure of a tank or other heavy object impacting on the upper surface of the mine.

All we could do was to look at one another.

Anyone of us could have stepped on the mine and we would have been blown to bits. The angels had to be working overtime up in Heaven looking after us.

All of us were very grateful that they were.

Chapter 28

Fate's Folly

Marina di Pisa, Italy, 1945

At the mouth of the Arno River, the fishermen rig large mesh nets on timber frames that extend quite a ways over the water.

The massive fishing nets are then released deep into the river by using an intricate system of pulleys. When they are quickly hauled up out of the water, the resulting catch of fish is very impressive and usually varied to include large and small varieties of fish and a generous amount of shrimp, small crabs, calamari, and some eel mixed in.

Most of the nearby restaurants along the waterfront which were run by the wives of these fishermen tended to feature caciucco, a robust seafood stew as their most popular main dish. Its thick broth included generous chunks of fresh onion, crushed garlic and ripe, plump tomatoes. The flavorful dish contained the very fruit of the sea, and was offered to the four of us in large bowls and accompanied by platters of oven-fresh, grilled, country garlic bread which had the pungent aroma of garlic deeply rubbed through nearly every crusty portion.

The main dish was also seasoned with a considerable amount of dried red peppers, so the consumption of more than a few glasses of the local red wine was not only a fine accompaniment to the meal, but also a true necessity.

John, Tina, Rina and I looked forward to this same delicious meal in the late afternoon sun almost every evening we were together those final days in Marina di Pisa.

Rina and John were busy helping the local fishermen unload their daily catch, when Tina turned to ask me when I thought my Army unit might return to the United States.

Tina could see that I was struggling to provide her with a brief, meaningful answer to a very difficult question. The exact date of my unit's immediate departure for the United States was expected soon, and when my commanders did issue orders, they did so under the veil of operational secrecy and the entire unit would then deploy quickly as ordered.

She acknowledged that the precious love we had shared could soon be torn away from us with little if any notice.

I felt she had a right to know when I would leave.

I prayed that the Army would offer me at least some form of advance notice when the time came to share with her. I prayed to myself that they would.

"Tina, I want you to know something," I said to her.

"I'm coming back here. We can't just leave one another like this. There's more to it."

She gently touched my hand.

"I love you, but please remember Burke, that I'm still married."

I didn't care about what possible problems might stand in our way, or what we might face when I did, in fact, return after the war.

"You'll get a divorce."

"In Italy, there's no such thing."

"Then we'll go some place else where you'll get one, perhaps Switzerland, or maybe France."

"Burke, I'm afraid you're just being a dreamer."

"You know things will be difficult for us in Italy after the war."

"Who knows what can happen?"

"Tina, don't you want me to come back to you?"

"Yes, my love, I do. More than anything else I know. I also want things to be good for you, too. First, promise me you will see how things are in your country before deciding to come back here, to Italy. You will write me everything. We will see."

Tina sighed and looked out toward the waters of the Arno River.

"You know, one time Rina asked me if I thought you would ever come back to me again. That was the first time you went up to Loiano. I told Rina I felt that someone had sent you to me, to help me through a life that, until I met you, I had found unbearable and unhappy. Maybe it was my mother, I don't really know.

"I told Rina that I was certain I would see you again."

"And now what do you think?" I asked, taking her palm in mine. "Do you think you will see me again if I leave for the United States?"

Tears welled in Tina's eyes.

"I want to say yes, but for the very first time, I'm terribly afraid."

"Don't be afraid, Tina. There's nothing to fear but fear itself."

The quote had worked for our late President, Franklin D. Roosevelt at the start of the war and was the only positive comment I could think of that might reassure her at that moment. My words made her laugh and brought us through the pain neither one of us wanted to confront at that moment.

Tina and I held one another close as we walked together towards the banks of the Arno River where Rina and John then stood.

We then walked slowly up to the little footbridge where we made our plans for the next day. Tina and Rina would travel by bicycle to meet us near the location of an old stone church that dated back to ancient Roman times and we would enjoy one last afternoon outing together. The Army had been taking their sweet time to ship us home, so John and I felt we deserved to take full advantage of any free time we might be offered.

I took Tina by the arm.

"That Catholic church sounds like something that should not be missed. Maybe we could get married there some day."

Tina smiled at me.

"You know you're a real dreamer, Burke, and a little crazy too."

"Of course, I am. I love you!"

I took Tina tenderly in my arms and softly kissed her lips.

"Don't forget we have a date someday in that church."

Our evening meal was good for a change, and the movie we stopped to see that evening was a wonderful romantic escape for each of us.

The film we saw was "Cover Girl," a 1944 Technicolor musical starring Rita Hayworth and Gene Kelly which featured some spectacular musical numbers, including "Long Ago and Far Away" and later became well known for Kelly's famous "alter-ego" dance in which he appeared to be actually dancing with himself.

We had each seen so few recent American movies during the war years that almost anything was worth seeing. The prominent title song in the movie, with lyrics by Ira Gershwin and music by Jerome Kern felt like it had been written especially for us.

"Long ago and far away, I dreamed a dream one day
And now that dream is here beside me
Long the skies were overcast
But now the clouds have passed
You're here at last!
Chills run up and down my spine
Aladdin's Lamp is mine
The dream I dreamed was not denied me

> *Just one look and then I knew*
> *That all I longed for*
> *Long ago was you."*

When Tina and I returned late that evening to Rina's aunt's home, we were exhausted emotionally and went quietly to bed.

Chapter 29

"That's it, kid"

Montecatini Staging Area, Italy

On the drive back to the 196th Signal Photo Company main garrison at Montecatini, I wondered aloud if I would ever have another opportunity to be able to see Tina before I shipped out for the United States.

I couldn't help but now think of Tina; her smile, and the sweet taste of our last kiss on my lips. I knew our remaining time together was rapidly running out.

I unlaced each of my boots, undressed and settled into my bunk for what little measure of sleep I thought I might be able to enjoy before facing morning formation.

I tried to close my eyes and relax. My body was just too damn restless to even consider sleep.

My trembling fingers soon drew an unfiltered cigarette from the opened pack I left outside in my unbuttoned shirt pocket.

The interior of my field tent was briefly bathed in bright light by the crisp, quick flick of my Zippo lighter. Swirling cigarette smoke moved upwards in lazy spirals through the stale air surrounding me. I smoked one down to the crushed nub, and then another.

The late evening air in my Army field tent was filled with the annoying swarming buzz of marauding mosquitoes at play, the constant cacophony of crickets, and the deeper, snoring sounds of slumbering soldiers certainly now dreaming of home. None of their heads and hearts were so heavily filled with such thoughts of despair as mine was now.

Morning sunlight bathed a long, winding column of half-awake, barely dressed soldiers steadily shuffling forward with mess trays in hand waiting their turn to enjoy the great breakfast delicacy, chipped beef on toast, politely known to the uninitiated as shit on a shingle, or "S.O.S."

John Mason sat with me, drinking hot coffee, when the urgent sounds of the overhead public address system announced that formation would be called immediately after breakfast and everyone had better be there on the double.

My last sip of hot, bitter coffee nearly gagged me. I cleared my throat and looked up to find John's eyes fixed squarely on mine.

"I'm afraid that's it, kid," he said.

"Jesus, John, I hope for once, you're wrong."

John wasn't wrong.

Our commanding officer, Captain Ned Morehouse, told us at formation we would depart the area at 10:00 o'clock that morning on July 4, 1945. The orders we were given by him were clear and precise.

The 196th Signal Photo Company would first proceed by truck convoy to the Livorno Port of Embarkation (POE) and then embark onboard the Army Transportation Service transport ship USAT Henry Gibbins, at a date to be later announced, to get underway to return to the United States.

None of us had much time for anything after chow than to pack our remaining personal gear, and then leave.

To leave unexpectedly is certainly not the worst thing in the world, but doing so when someone you love is standing on a street waiting without ever knowing what really happened, is an exercise in pure hell for both sides.

My only mildly comforting thought was that Tina would know by my sudden absence that the inevitable had finally happened.

Preparing for departure from Montecatini was of little or no effort since most of our things had long been packed away in our individual barracks bags. Only our personal remaining daily necessities were to be packed in a musette bag, For once, we weren't going to be carrying our full bedrolls, blankets and cots this time.

The Army Transportation Corps who was handling our cruise home would certainly see to it that once onboard, we were going home snug and comfortable.

General Dwight D. Eisenhower, Supreme Commander of the Allied Expeditionary Forces, had issued a directive that his victorious soldiers returning to the States should have a first-class ride home. Maybe it was Ike's own way of settling some old gripes so many of our guys had about their time in the service or the way they got to the front lines.

Our truck convoy departed right on schedule and we soon headed towards the Italian coast in the eventual direction of Pisa. Dozens of canvas-covered two and a half ton trucks each filled to capacity with soldiers and their gear began to roll steadily forward.

John and I climbed in and took our seats near the rear tailgate watching as the trucks who followed us struggled to keep pace. The lengthy, military convoy would suddenly jerk forward, forcing all of us to unexpectedly tumble like dominos from our seats, and then for no apparent reason would abruptly stop, setting us back in place once more.

When the truck convoy eventually merged onto the main highway, we could see the famous Leaning Tower of Pisa, the prominent front of the cathedral complex, and the dome of the Baptistery shining brightly in the afternoon sun as we drew steadily near.

It was only weeks ago the Piazza dei Miracoli that my friends John, Rina, Tina and I had enjoyed a memorable afternoon together. I never thought that such a prominent landmark would ever play such an important role in my adult life.

In my mind's eye, I could see the whole route we would travel; straight down Highway 1, then past Tombolo and then on to the coast route around the city and into the Leghorn port area.

When we crossed the now rusting, Bailey bridge which spanned the Arno River, something miraculous happened.

We took a sharp right and I could see the whole convoy was now going towards the Marina di Pisa.

John grabbed my arm and motioned in the direction. The scene was too much for either one of us to imagine.

John and I would be traveling through Marina di Pisa and it would be near enough to the scheduled time of our date with Tina and her friend Rina.

Our arrival time was just enough, but still, I thought too early. I felt a little push of hope from someone up there that we could keep our date together.

We passed the familiar fishing nets and then turned into the town. Our convoy had to reduce its speed through the center of the downtown area, and I looked ahead to the place of our scheduled rendezvous and saw no one waiting there.

The lyrics to the song, "Lili Marlene" came to mind as Lili waited under the lamplight near the barracks wall in vain for the soldier she loved to arrive.

I saw Tina and Rina purposely walk out of the only bakery in that end of town and I immediately leaned out from the rear of the truck towards them and called their names.

The convoy suddenly did another one of those strange slow downs.

Both Tina and Rina ran toward the street, their bread falling from their sacks along the way. Rina stopped at the edge of the road. Tina continued to run after the truck extending both her hands towards me. I reached out for it without success.

"Gatto, good-bye.

Remember I love you. I will wait for you. Write me with your news..."

"I will, and I love you, Tina.

I'll be back. Please remember that."

The truck now gained speed as it cleared the few buildings on both sides of the roadway which remained.

"Tina go back, you'll be hurt."

I thought of Romeo and the last words he said to his dear Juliet.

"Eyes, look your last! Arms, take your last embrace!"

Tina had loosened her grasp on the truck's webbed tailgate strap which she reached instead of my hand.

I could see her pace now quickening in an attempt to keep up with that of the truck.

"Goodbye Gatto," she exclaimed.

"Please come back!"

At that moment, I hated the guys in back of the Army truck which I was riding with for the comments they were now making about Tina.

I shouted back towards her.

"I will be back. I love you. Please let go. You'll hurt yourself."

She finally let go of the strap as the lumbering, 2-1/2 ton Army truck steadily gained speed. Tina now stood behind in the distance waving at me.

Tears were streaming down her face. Further back I could also see Rina waving at the truck.

I could not believe what was now happening to me. It felt like a sad scene in a movie I had seen long ago.

Tina stood beside the road sobbing like a child who had lost her favorite toy. She had. She had lost her Blue Cat.

It was over.

That was our finish, almost one year to the day when we first met.

I felt John's comforting hand on my shoulder, but I couldn't look at him.

I found it too difficult to see.

My eyes were still full of flowing tears.

Tina was still there, only now further back in the distance.

The dreaded moment we always knew one day would happen to us, had finally happened.

We had exchanged so many goodbyes in our year together; many possible last embraces each and every time I headed to the front lines that for now, this farewell would be the final one.

This was truly our last farewell.

Epilogue

Coming home to Italy at last

July 1945

I never stopped thinking about Tina and the love we shared together throughout the monotonous, twelve-day voyage home to the United States.

I vividly remember trying to feel the same sense of joy I saw in the faces of returning servicemen who painted beautiful pictures to me of their loving wives, sweethearts, children and parents they left back home. I just couldn't. I quietly kept to myself for most of the voyage home, trying to fight back the inevitable tears that would always come.

I tried so hard to be brave as I left Tina, the love of my life, sadly behind as our military truck convoy rolled out of her sight towards the Leghorn Port of Embarkation.

I didn't now know how Tina would ever manage to see her beloved "Gatto" again.

I knew deep in my heart that I would try to return. I had to.

The lights would come on "all over the world" as we so hopefully sang when the world war finally ended.

I hoped and I prayed as the transport ship got underway on July 14, 1945 to cross the Atlantic Ocean towards the United States, that the bloody war in the Pacific would end before my unit the 196th Signal Photo Company would be deployed there.

None of us onboard, as happy as many members of the 196th said they were to be at last heading home early in the summer of 1945 honestly knew what the Army had planned for us. We were each allowed to take personal leave not soon after our arrival on July 25, 1945, but were required to return to our temporary Army duty station, Fort Dix, New Jersey.

The consequences of two atomic bombs dropped on the Japanese cities of Nagasaki and Hiroshima in early August 1945 sealed the fate of the Japanese war machine once and for all.

I quietly signed my Army DD-214 discharge at Fort Dix, New Jersey on September 4, 1945 where I originally reported for basic training and received my final mustering out pay in the amount of $184.17 from the paymaster. I also said farewell to my former partner, Don Wiedenmayer who was also discharged from the Army on the same day at Ft. Dix and many more members of the 196th SPC who had become my friends and would now walk on "civvy street" at long last.

Free from the U.S. Army, I happily walked through the post's main gates back into civilian life and I didn't look back.

I returned by train to New York City's Grand Central Station, found a temporary place to stay, and soon talked by telephone to a few close family and friends while I set out on the real task of applying for an official U.S. passport to get back to Italy.

What now, I wondered?

What else could possibly stand in my way of being able to board heading back to Italy, back into Tina's arms, where I knew I belonged?

While the post-war world seemed to be getting somewhat back to normal, the process of obtaining an official U.S. Passport was an entirely different matter. Approval of my passport application wasn't anyone's bureaucratic priority.

Through a priest friend I got to a high ranking official in the New York State Democratic Party. He had a long outstanding debt from an attractive Miss Shipley, the Passport Division Chief for a personal favor he had performed for her years before. The favor had to do with her private life, nothing official. Miss Shipley had told him that he had only to ask for whatever she could do. So the priest asked her for me and within ten days, I had the small, green U.S. passport I needed that said I was going to Italy on "business affairs of a private nature."

I happily boarded a former Liberty transport ship docked in Baltimore harbor that was carrying a cargo of bulk grain to the port of Sicily. After a series of not-to-be-forgotten travel adventures in a country still on its heels from the recent war, I was once again back in the city of Florence and home where I knew I truly belonged.

I remember riding on the top of the only municipal bus going in the general direction of the small village of Colli Alti not far from where the Villa Calamai was located and feeling my heart beat steadily faster with the sight of each and every now familiar landmark that drew me so much closer to Tina at long last.

And at last, there I was.

I saw Tina before she saw me.

She looked ever so beautiful as she gazed into the bright, colorful petals of her rose garden, tending to each flower so carefully, not knowing I was now standing at that moment just steps away from her.

I dropped my bags and just ran towards her.

I felt the warmth of her lips on mine as I held her close.

Our love blossomed all over again, just as I had hoped it would, and we began the first moments of our new lives together once more.

Post-war Italy received a generous amount of humanitarian and financial aid from the United States and it wasn't long before the nation's economy had begun to show signs of steady recovery.

Tina and I marveled at the talent, skills and exquisite artisanship of proud Italian craftsmen, long the nation's greatest natural resource, who could be seen carefully restoring each and every historic treasure that had felt the destruction and trauma of the recent war.

Sadly, Tina's father, Signore Raffaello, passed away in 1948, and I was happy to comfort her at such a difficult time. While traveling to the beautiful city of Milan a few years later, we were equally saddened to see our good friend Rina, who had then been suffering from the effects of heart disease, pass away in Milan in 1952.

Tina and I sat together one afternoon in the very same restaurant near the fishing nets at Marina di Pisa where we exchanged our first wartime farewell. The restaurant had by then, become like so many others in the post-war recovery, a popular "in" place with fresh, new modern architecture, and accompanying higher meal prices.

Tina looked deeply into my eyes without even saying a word. I wondered where her thoughts at that moment had carried her.

"I always feel that this is really our place." The tone of Tina's voice deepened.

"Here. It was right here, Burke, that I really believed deep in my heart, you would come back to me."

I clasped her hand in return as I replied.

"It's also the place of our last 'addio.' That evening was the saddest moment of my life; I didn't know if I had lost you forever."

I then explained to Tina that I had made a vow to her which I intended to keep.

"Before I left, I told you I would never leave you ever again. And I never will."

Her eyes brimming with tears, Tina asked, "You never have been sorry?"

I had heard those cautious words whispered from Tina's lips several times before. She had wondered aloud whether I had any lingering doubts or personal regrets in deciding so urgently to leave the United States upon my discharge from the Army just to come back to Italy to be with her.

I had none. I put her concerns gently to rest each time she raised them.

I simply loved Tina with all my heart and soul. Nothing else could or would ever matter. We had been blessed by whatever divine spirits that had brought our hearts and lives together.

"I would go through the war all over again, Tina, if I thought you would be waiting for me at the end of it."

"But then, Burke, you would have to leave me once again."

I thought for a brief moment, taking her hands tenderly in mine as we each prepared to leave what had become in the city of Pisa, a very special place of memories.

"You're right, Tina," I replied.

"Let's just leave it the way it is. I like it better this way."

In Italy, I enjoyed a satisfying new career in federal civil service at Camp Darby, the Pisa Army Base and in time resumed a measure of the theatrical career I had started before the war in New York City, producing plays for base personnel and even working as an actor in the Italian film industry.

Our love did stand the test of time upon my return to Italy in 1946 for the next twenty-six beautiful years.

* * *

Afterword

Tina passed away in my arms in our penthouse apartment overlooking the sea in Livorno, in early June 1972 which had, beside the villa at Colli Alti, become our second home. I buried her beside her mother and father in Florence, a place Tina had always felt the necessity to go and vigorously breathe in some of the intense, wonderful atmosphere of metropolitan Florence, every now and then.

Tina had always suspected that she expected to die before me, since loneliness was not a quality in her opinion she felt I could again sufficiently handle. Tina had told me that should she pass away before me, she would want me to always cherish her memory, but actively consider returning to the United States.

I had always sensed Tina had a hidden, personal feeling of guilt for keeping me in Italy for her sake for so many years. Or, perhaps, maybe she truly knew how I might feel in Italy, once I was alone without her.

Without Tina, the beautiful, historic city of Florence we both had loved so much had become a lonely place.

Historic, beautiful Florence was the unlikely setting where the very dreams of both our young lives had first unfolded.

Our beautiful home, the Villa Calamai which we had each come to love so very much, now lost its embracing, comforting atmosphere. Its rooms became large and cavernous and at times, almost frightening to me without her.

I didn't want to admit it to myself, but maybe Tina was right after all.

It was time to leave after thirty years of a wonderful life in Florence, Italy, to return to the United States and begin a new life once again.

The journey which brought my stepfather Burke O'Connell back to the United States for the first time since 1946 is not described by him in his original memoir, nor are the circumstances which led him to be socially introduced to my mother, Jan Whitman in the city of West Los Angeles, California later in 1972.

What I do know is their initial friendship soon turned to love. My new stepfather, whom I had nicknamed, "my Irish pop" from a poem I wrote for him, married my mother and took our family back to Italy in 1974. We lived in the same penthouse apartment in Livorno which he had shared with his beloved Tina.

Burke then retraced for all of us what had been for him a wonderful, well-lived life before coming to the United States.

My parents' surprising decision to move our family to Italy and live in Burke's penthouse apartment where I would begin my junior year in high school sounded beyond my wildest imagination.

Burke concludes his original memoir in the initial setting where his story first began, in conversation with his good friend Heinz Himmelman, the owner of a Santa Monica, California art and framing gallery who framed many of his original oil paintings I now have in my own home in Pacifica, California.

Heinz held the uncoiled regimental citation for heroism open in his hands waiting for my answer. I quietly looked back at him to the faded, wrinkled scroll he held before offering my reply.

All I honestly did was cross the Arno River to get to the other side.

The path which unexpectedly led me to meet my beautiful Tina had to have been written in the stars.

The U.S. Army's citation was more than just an official document, and deserved a higher measure of personal recognition than being unceremoniously tucked out of sight in my desk drawer.

"Heinz, perhaps, for once, this really does deserve a special frame."

I sensed Heinz agreed, even though he had more questions about my former military service in Italy than I might ever have time to adequately answer for him.

Outside Heinz's Santa Monica, California, gallery, the warm afternoon sun bathed my face as I walked towards Palisades Park, not four blocks away, which overlooked the Pacific Ocean.

I thought of the thirty years that had now passed since the end of the war. I didn't realize I had lived longer in Italy than I had in my own native country. My memories of Tina and our wonderful life together in Italy would last all of my lifetime.

I remembered a brief verse taken from a modest book of poems Tina and I held dear at the Villa Calamai so many years ago.

Somehow, these tender words were still on my mind:

> **I hear a voice you cannot hear**
> **Which says I must not stay;**
> **I see a hand you cannot see**
> **Which beckons me away.**—*Colin and Lucy*
> Thomas Tickell

My mother, Jan, my brother, Jeff, me and Burke in a photo taken in early 1972—note Burke's snazzy jacket—taken at our first apartment complex in West Los Angeles by a family friend. Photo was taken before we all moved to Italy.

(O'Connell family photo)

Burke O'Connell and my mother, Jan standing in front of our fireplace in our luxurious penthouse in Livorno, Italy. The sequined gown my mother wears had once belonged to Tina Calamai.

(O'Connell family photo)

Burke O'Connell introduces our family to the historic Villa Calamai where his wartime relationship with Tina Calamai first began. Burke, my younger brother Jeff, my mother, Jan and I stand left to right beside an outside well near the front entrance. Casting shadows upon the front of the villa stands an immense fig tree just across the courtyard.

(O'Connell family photo)

Burke, my mother, Jan, myself (center) and my younger brother, Jeff in our family's luxurious penthouse apartment in the city of Livorno, Italy. My stepfather shared this same apartment with Tina for many years until her death in early 1972. The apartment, which overlooked the Tirranian Sea, was ornately decorated by Tina and Burke with many historic treasures from the Villa Calamai which they held dear.

(O'Connell family photo)

My stepfather, Burke holding my hand to congratulate me on my 1975 high school graduation. Throughout the years, Burke became more like a real father and less of a stepfather to me as he watched me mature into a woman with children of my own.
(O'Connell family photo)

Jeff, Jan, Julie and Julie's Viennese friend, Denise trying to pose like they're holding up the Leaning Tower of Pisa but they didn't elbow it in the correct way.
(O'Connell family photo)

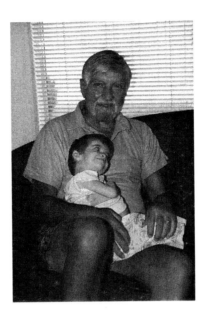

Burke with my firstborn son, Alexander Graham Jones, in my condo in Garden Grove, California. Burke became more like a grandfather to my children than my own biological father.

(O'Connell family photo)

A favorite, fun picture taken at our condo in Palm Springs of my brother Jeff, at left, Burke O'Connell, aglow in the center, and myself, at right. I always thought Burke was a saint!

(O'Connell family photo)

My mother, Jan, with Burke in the *Valley Player's Guild* production of "Fiddler on the Roof" performed in Palm Springs, California in the late 1970s. Burke took charge as Set Designer as well as acted with my mother in many of their productions.

(O'Connell family photo)

Burke gave me this jolly, little clown puppet as a Christmas present when we lived in Santa Monica, California. We named him Sunshine because he always brought a little bit of sunshine to our lives. Standing behind our Christmas tree is an antique black moor, one of the many historical artifacts we brought back from Italy.

(O'Connell family photo)

Burke, our dog, Pierre and my mom, Jan in Palm Springs, where our family moved to after living in Santa Monica, California.

(O'Connell family photo)

Burke loved to relax in the late afternoon and early evenings with his favorite pipe which usually held cherry-flavored tobacco which I purchased for him during the holidays. Here he is posing in his favorite denim jacket, looking rather distinguished, I might add.

(O'Connell family photo)

Mary Cassat's "The Boating Party" lovingly painted in oils by Burke in 1975 in Santa Monica, California where my family lived upon returning to the United States from Italy.

(Photo by Julie Whitman Jones)

A colorful cornflower meadow reveals a young man and woman, perhaps Tina and Burke who wave to one another upon reuniting after a long absence apart. Her parasol is tossed to the side as she calls out to him, longing to embrace him once more. This oil painting by Burke captures his remembrance of springtime in Colli Alti as the Villa Calamai is seen in the distant horizon.

(Photo by Julie Whitman Jones)

Burke reproduced a favorite Italian painting in this farm scene depicting three turkeys on a crisp Autumn day in the Italian countryside.

(Photo by Julie Whitman Jones)

Burke's 1972 Italian driver's license issued while he was a federal civil service employee at Camp Darby in Livorno, Italy.

(O'Connell collection)

Tina Calamai painted the exterior of the Villa Calamai in oils many years after the war. Her painting of the villa is displayed in the home of Jan Whitman-O'Connell McGuire in Palm Springs, California.
(Photo by Julie Whitman Jones)

Tina Calamai painted the interior furnishings of the Villa Calamai in Colli Alti as it looked following the war. The original oil painting is displayed in the home of Jan Whitman-O'Connell McGuire in Palm Springs, California.
(Photo by Julie Whitman Jones)

Celebrating with a glass of wine and a candle on a cupcake, Burke relaxes in his corduroy suit, happy to be surrounded by his family and friends.

(O'Connell family photo)

Burke, my second son, Grant Aramis Jones and my mom, Jan in my condo in Garden Grove, California. This photo was taken in August, 1988 when Grant was one month old. Burke died in December of that year.
(O'Connell family photo)

The United States of America
honors the memory of

EDMUND B. O'CONNELL

This certificate is awarded by a grateful nation in recognition of devoted and selfless consecration to the service of our country in the Armed Forces of the United States.

Ronald Reagan
President of the United States

Burke was honored for his military service in the Italian campaign in a presidential citation our family received in his remembrance.

(O'Connell collection)

Burke passed away during the Christmas holiday season which he loved so much, one month before his 75th birthday. He is buried at the Los Angeles National Cemetery, Los Angeles, California.

—*Photo by Los Angeles National Cemetery.*

Notes

Abbreviations Used In the Text

- APS   Army Pictorial Service
- OIC   Officer in Charge
- SCPC   Signal Corps Photographic Center (Army)
- SPC   Signal Photographic Company (Army)

Origins of the 196th Signal Photo Company

The 3131st Signal Service Company was formed in Algiers by Allied Force Headquarters (AFHQ) as a provisional unit. There was also an ongoing need in Allied Force Headquarters for both still and motion picture photographers, as that was the hub and command center of the combined French, English and American effort in Sicily and in Italy.

Photographers Edmund Burke O'Connell and Donald Wiedenmayer served in the 3131st in North Africa and were made members of the 196th SPC in early 1945 when the unit was reorganized and redesignated.

Requests for photographic coverage of specific projects in Mediterranean Theater of Operations frequently came from Washington, D.C. and a specific team was assigned to cover a specific phase of combat operations.

In Italy the assignment came through the Photo Signal officer on the Army Signal Officers Staff.

In Italy this was Col. Melvin E. Gillette until he was replaced by Major Linden G. Rigby about the time the 163rd Signal Photo Company was transferred to the Seventh Army for the invasion of Southern France.

The Fifth Army was required to give up a considerable number of combat units to the Seventh Army in 1944 and the 163rd SPC was one of them. Photographers of the 163rd SPC provided significant photographic coverage of early combat operations in Italy until their reassignment.

When General Mark Clark became 15th Army Group Commander in late 1944 and wanted photo coverage of the Italian campaign the 3131st was ordered into the Italian theater to join the 163rd SPC.

Many of the officers and men who were attached to the 163rd SPC in Italy were relieved and were temporarily reassigned to the 3131st bringing their equipment with them. One member of the 3131st, photographer Harry B. Morgan, is on a personnel roster of the 163rd and then again on the 196th SPC.

According to the unit's historical records and those of its last commanding officer, Captain Ned Morehouse, the 3131st was not administratively organized for purpose of providing combat coverage in Italy. The 3131st simply lacked the appropriate number of trained men and officers necessary to accomplish its mission.

Fifth Army orders were prepared on February 24, 1945 transferring each individual by name, MOS, and rank to the newly-designated 196th SPC whereupon the 3131st was deactivated, and the 196th was simultaneously activated. The transfer process was accomplished in a single order which took three days to type up.

The 196th SPC was attached to the Fifth Army during the closing months of the Italian campaign; from activation date until June 1, 1945, when it returned to Montecatini for redeployment to the United States.

Donald Wiedenmayer, photographer

Don Wiedenmayer, 89, retired on Dec. 31, 1978 after completing 21 years as photographer with the Vermont Department of Highways, now known as the Vermont Agency of Transportation. This date coincided with his completion of a career of over 41 years of professional photography.

Don and his wife Shirley are the proud parents of three daughters and have enjoyed pleasantly spending the past twenty New England winters (1983-2003) in sunny Cocoa Beach, Florida. He continues to be an avid photographer and while in Florida enjoyed photographing many of our nation's manned space shuttle launches.

Wiedenmayer graduated from the Clarence H. White School of Photography in New York in 1937 and was engaged as an advertising photographer in New York City while operating his own studio at 6 E. 46th Street.

During World War II, Don served in the Army Pictorial Service as a war photographer in England, North Africa and Sicily. He participated as a newsreel photographer in the invasion of North Africa, and took part in five Mediterranean Theater campaigns.

After the war, Don lived in New York City from 1945 to 1948 while working for the Robert E. Coates Studio and the advertising department photographic studio of the Eastman Chemical Products Corporation, a subsidiary of Eastman Kodak.

Don moved to Wallingford, Vermont in 1948 where he produced advertising photography for Vermont Industries and in 1958 joined the Vermont Department of Highways as a highway photographer. He later managed the Department's photographic section and took photographs for right of way, construction, traffic, bridge, aerial, planning, materials and public information uses.

Wiedenmayer is a past president of the Vermont Professional Photographers in 1952-53 and 1969-70 and is a former member of the Professional Photographers of America.

He and his wife make their home in Worcester, Vermont.

HEADQUARTERS
196th SIGNAL PHOTOGRAPHIC COMPANY
CAMP GRUBER, OKLAHOMA

26 October 1945

SUBJECT: Histories of Subordinate Units

TO: The Adjutant General
War Department
Washington, D.C.
(THRU CHANNELS)

1. The 196th Signal Photographic Company under direction of Army Pictorial Service became activated on 24 February 1945 at Trespiano, Italy. Was composed of 17 Officers, 1 Warrant Officer, and 130 Enlisted Men, and was under the command at that time of Captain Ned. R. Morehouse.
2. A photographic company is unique in its operation as their coverage on a wide front makes it both possible and necessary for all of its combat photo teams to act, for the most part, as their own. That is to say, while there are certain missions to cover, the photographers are at liberty to go as far as they like, of course, always keeping in mind that a "dead" photographer is worth very little to his organization. Only when a man can go up, get the pictures and return, is his value to the unit put to best advantage.
3. The 196th was attached to the Fifth Army during the closing months of the Italian campaign; from activation date on 24 February 1945 to 1 June 1945 when it returned to Montecatini for redeployment to the United States.
4. The mission of this command was to gather both still and motion pictures. The pictures to be secured were of many varieties. While their primary objective was to secure pictures of combat, the various missions entailed all types of record, historical, publicity, strategic and others of a morale-building nature. The company had a laboratory, which moved constantly with the organization itself and a well set-up headquarters personnel which had to keep the forward elements of the command teams always supplied with materials and necessities to aid them in completing their hazardous missions. For instance, in keeping the vehicles always ready for their difficult journeys through rough terrain. Seeing the food, PX supplies, changes of clothing and photographic supplies were ever on

hand. The Headquarters camera repair department had to have the cameras always in top condition. This was particularly difficult due to the many miles that separated the photo combat teams and the headquarters of these teams.

5. The Company was set up in such a way that there was one photo liaison officer with each Corps of the Army. At this time under Fifth Army, the 196th, with its Army Pictorial Service officer at Fifth Army HQ operated under IV Corps and II Corps. From these corps the liaison officers delegated teams, averaging six for each Corps, composed of one still man, one motion picture man and one driver, and assigned to the various Divisions on the line at the time. From then on each team worked separately, most of the time living at Battalion or Division Headquarters or whatever suitable housing was possible to protect their valuable equipment. Seeing that the equipment was maintained in perfect running order was a prerequisite to all other requirements. Working closely with Division CP's these teams found out where the best material was to be found and where to go to secure it. The team would then proceed down through Regiment, Battalion, Company and even platoon if there was sufficient safety to make the pictures and yet return with them.

6. There were many problems to consider. One of them was the difficult terrain over which the teams traveled and the absolute necessity of getting their pictures back to Corps. After all, old pictures, of a particular news and noteworthy occasion are of no value if too late to tie in with the news of that particular sector engaged at the time. Getting the pictures to Corps, then flown back to rear laboratories and processed and flown to the States after censorship, was carried on with the least possible delay. Another thing was the constant traveling forward and backward under constant enemy fire. However, due to the set-up of the organization where it worked closely in touch with all echelons of the Division it was assigned to, the teams performed their work with speed and efficiency.

7. One of the most hazardous and yet most important duties was that of oblique terrain photography for the S-3's of the Divisions. This work was little known to the general public and yet was a key function in the final stages of the Italian Campaign. From these terrain photos Divisions worked out their overlays, artillery used them for plotting and the enlarged prints were valuable all the way down to the platoon in determining patrol action or counter measures against enemy positions. The work done by the 196th in terrain photo work was highly praised by Major General V.E. Prichard, the Commanding Officer of the 1st Armored Division and by Fifth Army Lieutenant General Lucian K. Truscott himself, besides the individual commendations by many of the Division officers. This work was carried

on extensively for the 91st, 85th, 88th, 34th and 1st Armored Divisions during their actions in the North Apennine Mountains south of Bologna.

8. It is important to note here that the cameramen as brought into the company were pleased where their particular qualifications could do the most good. A good news man, who acted as such in civilian life, was sent to forward areas, where after being broken in by the men already a long time in the combat zone, would relieve another man in need of rest or a change of sector. Some cameramen remained in rear areas for PRO work and the other photo necessities and at the same time became more aware of the combat work going on in case they were required to join a combat team. The motion picture men saw rushes periodically of their work and the still men received back any culled negatives and both received periodic critiques on their work to keep abreast of improvements and recommendations. Thousands of feet of movie film shot was used by the major newsreel companies, the Signal Corps films such as Screen Magazine and Combat Bulletins and other specially prepared films like "San Pietro", "Army Nurse," "Cub Pilot", and many other vital films both an aid to training and also of general public interest. The pictures made by the still men were used extensively by all major photographic syndicates and newspapers, Yank Magazine, ETO newspapers and hundreds of other publications.

9. It was in the last stages of the Italian campaign, which extended from driving the Germans out of the Apennines, across the Po Valley to their final surrender in the foothills of the Alps. It was a proper meeting when members of the 196th of the Fifth Army and the 163rd of the Seventh Army joined hands across Brenner Pass in the Alps. Some of the outstanding photography of the war was accomplished in the engagements driving the enemy out of the mountains south of Bologna and their utter retreat across the Po Valley and our own speedy chase, including the crossing of the Po River. During these days of a speedily moving front, the photo teams had great difficulty in covering the daily action, returning with it to Corps Headquarters and catching up with the forward elements the same night or the following morning. However, this was done and the first pictures of Bologna is an outstanding example, as the photographs made by members of the 196th were rushed to Fifth Army rear a full 10 hours before any other organization or other cameramen were able to get back with pictures of the fall of this city. It was this way during the final days when the public in America were daily getting a graphic photographic account of the retreat of the German forces in Italy.

10. But the job did not end there. As the occupation work grew and war criminals were being sought out, the camera teams were still working

with the Divisions. Going on CIC raids, covering occupation work and recording for history all the intricate details even the written word could not secure.

11. In the meantime the Company Headquarters had moved from Trespiano, Italy, to Verona in order to be able to serve their combat teams over an entire front from Trieste to Genoa along the entire Austrian and French border. However, on 1 June 1945 the 196th was recalled from active duty with the Fifth Army, to be one of the first units for indirect redeployment to the Pacific. This meant, with a tough fight still going on in the Pacific, the 196th would be rushed to the States for a 30-day rest and then on to the Pacific theatre.

12. On 1 June 1945 the organization set up quarters at Montecatini, Italy and began staging for their redeployment. On 5 July 1945 the 196th arrived at the PBS staging area, Pisa, Italy, and bivouacked while awaiting passage to America. They went aboard the USAT Henry Gibbons at Livorno, Italy for embarkation on 12 July 1945. They left the port of Livorno 14 July 1945 and arrived at Camp Patrick Henry, Virginia, 25 July 1945 where the men went to their respective reception centers for their 30 days recuperation and rest before assembling again at Camp Gruber, Oklahoma.

13. On 27 July 1945 the 196th Headquarters was set up at Camp Gruber, Oklahoma, and they began POM training for overseas deployment on 10 September 1945. First Lieutenant Franklin Cave assumed command on 25 September 1945 and the 196th Signal Photographic Company became inactivated 2 November 1945.

/s/ FRANKLIN CAVE
1St Lt., C.M.P.
Commanding

196th Signal Photo Company
Florence, Italy
1944-45

Still Photo Coverage

Last Name	First Name	Quantity Sept.-Dec.	Caption	News Value or Subject Coverage	Print Quality
Baker	Charles C.	123	87%	87%	87%
Bull	Marshall H.	47*	80%	90%	95%
Edwards	Robert G.	217	82%	87%	83%
Emery	(not listed)	24*	90%	84%	80%
Getty	George H.	135	81%	86%	85%
Graning	Paul D.	179	81%	84%	85%
Hartman	(not listed)	156	80%	95%	90%
Houghton	(not listed)	40*	81%	83%	85%
Kosseff	Jerome W.	168	81%	84%	84%
Levine	Melvin	221	75%	83%	80%
Mason	John T.	80	82%	85%	82%
McQuarrie	Donald G.	175	86%	85%	81%
McWhirter	William D.	96	78%	80%	85%
Mulcahy	John J.	154	80%	89%	84%
Peters	(not listed)	118*	70%	90%	90%
Phillips	Daniel P.	120	76%	84%	77%
Rusbar	Chester G.	62*	70%	93%	92%
Schmidt	Robert H.	380	76%	90%	88%
Tacey	Robert F.	170	81%	84%	84%
Thomas	Ralph E.	512	88%	92%	88%
Walden	(not listed)	35*	85%	85%	85%
Wiedenmayer	Donald	61*	83%	82%	80%
Yaskell	Peter	46	80%	90%	89%
Zube	Frank B.	176	79%	83%	83%

* Other duties

196th Signal Photo Company
Florence, Italy
1944-1945

Motion Picture Footage
(total feet)

As of December 19, 1944

First Name	Last Name	Sept	Oct.	Nov.	Dec.	Total
Martin G.	Brooks	1,300	800	600	800	3,500
Max	Campbell*	3,500	4,300	1,700	to 14 Nov. 44	10,500
Louis R.	Cook	2,100	1,100	500	**	3,700
Robert E.	Daley	6,650	1,800	1,200	200	9,850
Harry C.	Kreider	9,300	3,400	1,200	1,700	15,600
David D.	Kurland	100	500	**	1,100	1,700
(not listed)	Long	2,600	1,300	3,500	1,000	8,400
(not listed)	Mayer		1,050	400	500	1,950
Francis P.	Mulhair	1,640	2,200	200	800	4,840
Louis J. Jr.	Murchio	3,500	**	2,100	**	5,600

*   Killed by German bombing

Roll of Honor
196th Signal Photo Company

An informal typed unit roster of the 196th SPC furnished by Donald Wiedenmayer and a second embarkation roster of personnel dated July 6, 1945 are compiled into a listing of known still and motion picture photographers. Unit personnel are identified by rank, first and last name where possible. Any omissions by the author(s) are entirely unintentional.

Rank	Last Name	First Name
Officers		
Captain	Morehouse	Ned R.
1st Lt.	Ager	Edward R.
1st Lt.	Cave	Franklin
1st Lt.	Falcone	Phillip F.
1st Lt.	Harrington	John
1st Lt.	Morang	Frank L.
1st Lt.	Peterson	Earl T.
1st Lt.	Walter	Earl L.
1st Lt.	Wever	John S.
2nd Lt.	Emrich	Walter R. Jr.
2nd Lt.	Kreider	Harry C.
2nd Lt.	Lees	David B.
2nd Lt.	Leviton	Jay B.
2nd Lt.	Mulhair	Francis P.
2nd Lt.	Murchio	Louis J. Jr.
2nd Lt.	Schmidt	Robert H.
2nd Lt.	Tacey	Robert F.
Enlisted Men		
1st Sgt.	Baker	Charles
M Sgt.	Mulcahy	John J.
T. Sgt.	Daly	Robert E.
T.Sgt.	**Campbell**	**Cecil Max**
Staff Sgt.	Corey	Roger B.
Staff Sgt.	Crane	Roger B.

Staff Sgt.	Jones	Gordon
Staff Sgt.	Kurland	David D.
Staff Sgt.	Markman	Martin
Staff Sgt.	Spallucci	Joseph
Staff Sgt.	Stewart	David R.
Staff Sgt.	Thomas	Ralph E.
Tech 3	Cisler	Herny J.
Tech 3	Coffman	Charles
Tech 3	Cook	Louis R.
Tech 3	Elson	Saul
Tech 3	McWhirter	William D.
Tech 3	Rubin	Jack
Tech 3	Wiedenmayer	Donald
Sgt.	Gearhart	John H.
Sgt.	Klein	Howard F.
Sgt.	Kosseff	Jerome W.
Sgt.	Tischler	Samuel T.
Sgt.	Yung	Ben L.
Tech 4	Blosser	Robert D.
Tech 4	Bull	Marshall H.
Tech 4	Carlson	Ralph E.
Tech 4	Collins	Lloyd F.
Tech 4	Dunn	Everett H.
Tech 4	Getty	George H.
Tech 4	Graning	Paul D.
Tech 4	Hibler	Calvin E.
Tech 4	Kendrick	Robert M.
Tech 4	Lambert	Joseph H.
Tech 4	Levine	Melvin
Tech 4	Litt	Norman K.
Tech 4	Mason	John T.
Tech 4	McQuarrie	Donald G.
Tech 4	Melkonian	Melkon T.

Tech 4	**Morgan**	**Harry B.**
Tech 4	O'Connell	Edmund B.
Tech 4	Parthemos	James
Tech 4	Phillips	Daniel P.
Tech 4.	Rusbar	Chester G.
Tech 4.	Spirito	Severino F.
Tech 4.	Zube	Frank B.
Cpl.	Sandor	Albert J.
Tech 5	Bergstrom	Canton A.
Tech 5	Berry	Earnest G.
Tech 5	Bronson	Roland L.
Tech 5	Brown	Albert L.
Tech 5	Fish	Edward H.
Tech 5	Gregg	Glenn W.
Tech 5	Hauser	Albert A.
Tech 5	Kaemmerer	Wilbert F.
Tech 5	Klapach	William S.
Tech 5	Mayer	Francis L.
Tech 5	Neiman	Jack
Tech 5	Owen	James M.
Tech 5	Pitts	Robert L.
Tech 5	Schilling	Carl F.
Tech 5	Shanks	William J.B.
Tech 5	Shepard	Francis L.
Tech 5	Stone	Francis A.
Tech 5	Thrift	Ernest N.
Tech 5	Tomszak	Eraz
Tech 5	White	Gilbert G.
Tech 5	Wisnoski	Roland J.

Army Photographer Killed at Fifth Army Front

A typed press release written by officers of the 3131st Signal Service Company and furnished by Donald Wiedenmayer who kept it to remember his good friend, was submitted for publication to Stars and Stripes (Mediterranean), Italy. The obituary recounts the life of T-Sgt. Cecil Max Campbell, 23, who became a chance victim of a Luftwaffe bomb.

WITH THE 5TH ARMY, Dec. 20, 1944 (Delayed)—One of the Mediterranean Theater's most respected combat cameramen is dead, victim of a chance Luftwaffe bomb. T-Sgt. Cecil M. "Max" Campbell had recorded action at Kasserine Pass, El Guettar and Gafsa in Tunisia.

Campbell and his newsreel camera jumped with the 82nd Airborne Division in Sicily. He was the only cameraman to go in with the amphibious assault behind the German lines at Santa Agata in Sicily. Again in Italy, the 23-year-old Scotsman from Mesa, Arizona saw it hot at Monte Cassino and Anzio.

With his heavy equipment, Campbell followed the 5th Army drives to Rome and Leghorn and then covered the rupture of the Gothic Line. All in all, he had spent two years as a combat cameraman.

Wounded once, he still considered himself lucky, although like all men who go into battle on their own initiative, he was fully conscious that the law of averages was running against him. Bedded down in a house several miles behind the front, he was buried under the rubble by an almost direct hit of a German Luftwaffe night bomber's stray missile.

A friend, Pvt. Nelson Pitts of Cleveland, Ohio was also buried but escaped serious injury. At the time of his death, Campbell was a member of the 3131st Signal Service Company, attached to the 5th Army.

Campbell was the sixth Army photographer to be killed in action in Italy, according to the Army Pictorial Service.

Donald Wiedenmayer's personal copy of a February 1945 Sunday *Stars and Stripes Magazine* news article describes the role of U.S. Army still and motion picture photographers in recording the Italian campaign of World War II. The article also featured a dramatic photo by photographer John Mulcahy of the 196th Signal Photo Company which can be found in the photo section.

Edmund Burke O'Connell is quoted in the article's final paragraphs describing the difficulties of filming in combat. The image and text of the article are reprinted with permission from *Stars and Stripes*.

Photo by APS: Behind the Familiar Photo Credit Line is Untold Story of GIs Recording Your War

By Sgt. STAN SWINTON
Staff Writer

WITH THE FIFTH ARMY—Photo editors thumbing through the daily grab bag of glossy prints one day last month might have gasped at a great photograph: the blossoming shrapnel of a German shell caught at the instant of fragmentation. It was the picture of the month, wire-photoed across America and reproduced in five-column enlargements by the nation's press.

The credit line was familiarly brief—"Signal Corps Photo." But behind it was the untold story of the anonymous cameramen who have brought home to American civilians the violence of modern war with an effectiveness that the most vivid words of war correspondents can never equal. That picture of a bursting shell, for instance, how did it come to be taken?

It began in the dreary Italian village of Loiano a week earlier when Pvt. Leonard Ryan of Clifton Heights, Pa., jockeyed his muddy jeep off Highway 65 and pulled up behind a building.

His passenger, photographer John Mulcahy of Chicago, clambered out to assist in lowering the windshield before continuing forward. Seconds later the first shell burst. Inside the building, where both had run for cover, Sgt. Mulcahy fumbled his Speed Graphic into adjustment. A second shell smashed into a church a few feet away. As the third hit, Sgt. Mulcahy was at the window. "Get the hell away from there," shouted Ryan. "I think I can get a shot of a shell burst." The prewar Chicago Tribune photographer replied imperturbably and moved to the open doorway. The seventh shell exploded 20 yards away and Mulcahy's shutter clicked at the second of impact. Then, waiting only long enough to make sure that a slightly-wounded GI could reach an aid station on his own, Mulcahy and Ryan climbed into their jeep and drove and walked up to the battle line to complete their original mission, terrain studies of enemy positions.

Such is the behind-the-scene story of just one of the 20,000 still photographs snapped in Italy by front-line Army Pictorial Service photographers last year. Add to that enough combat movies to make 700 full-length feature pictures plus an equal footage covering special productions or rear areas, and you can understand why military bigwigs believe the Italian campaign has been recorded on film with a thoroughness unsurpassed in military history.

Today the web of photographers covers the front and many rear areas. Skilled teams of still men, motion picture cameramen and expert drivers are attached to each division and corps of the 5th Army while others operate out of 15th Army Group, MTOUSA and the Peninsular Base Section. Special laboratories in Rome and Florence process their films swiftly.

The task of the Army Pictorial Service was five-fold. It was to convey information on combat and field operations to the War Department with war battle operations taking precedence. Photo information of immediate tactical and strategic value was to be secured for the theater commander. A complete photographic history of the war was necessary so that future students of tactics and strategy could observe what occurred in the primitive era of the 1940s. Staff agencies of both theater and War Department would call upon it for photographic data on the personnel, material conditions and new techniques. Lastly, APS was charged with meeting War Department requests for special productions intended for orientation, the record and public relations.

Army Pictorial Service itself was a paradox. It was the operational brains, but except for a handful of key administrators, its personnel belonged to Signal Photo Companies and similar units. Like most outfits, it suffered from confusion in the early days. Cameramen were sent to cover the North African invasion with inadequate two-inch lenses for still cameras and 16 rather than 35 mm movie cameras.

It was chiefly the photographic know-how of enlisted photographers and the energy of Col. Melvin E. Gillette, father of APS in this theater and former photo officer for AFHQ's Signal Section, which put APS into smooth operating order.

But it was the GI cameraman who did the work. Picture hungry, they moved along with the infantry in search of combat action. There was Pfc. Morris J. Schimmel of St. Louis, Mo., who was struck in the arm by shrapnel as he crouched beside a tank. He kept taking pictures until the movie camera spring ran down, then collapsed. T-Sgt. Cecil Max Campbell jumped with the paratroopers in Sicily and came down in an olive tree in time to see a second chute bearing his camera disappear over the horizon. Despite a sprained ankle, he joined the paratroops and fought his way to the Allied lines—but didn't make a single photo. When Monte Cassino was to be bombed, APS photographers bullied Big Bertha—a giant camera with a 40-inch lens—to a point where "we were looking down the necks of the Germans." Before daylight they camouflaged both camera and themselves. *Life Magazine* called their photo of MAAF's mass bombing next day "the outstanding picture of the war."

Living close to danger, the cameramen have suffered casualties. Last year five were killed among them T-Sgt. Campbell. Another 21 were wounded. The cost was high. The results?

"Every phase of the Italian Campaign has been recorded in pictures," reports Maj. Linden G. Rigby, 5th Army Photo Officer who went from the infantry to Hollywood after the last war. "The Italian veteran can look forward to seeing four movies running from 20 to 25 reels on his deeds. One covers Salerno to the Volturno, another the Volturno to Cassino, a third from Cassino to Rome and a fourth Rome to the Gothic Line."

Since last April, the Army Pictorial Service has devoted much of its energy to a little publicized activity—taking panoramic pictures of the front. With these minute photo studies before them, patrol observation posts and troops going into attack can operate with a precision unequalled in the past.

"Those terrain studies are the most important thing we're doing," reports Lt. Frank L. Morang. A veteran of 25 years in the movie business, Morang was sailing around the Gulf of Mexico "minding my own damn business" when the war broke out. He photographed the North African campaign as a private, and later won a commission.

Discussing panoramic shots of enemy front-line positions is considerably easier than getting them, since machine pistols don't distinguish between the cameramen and the infantrymen. APS photographers must go up to the most forward observation posts or positions to get their shots. Often they make the trip forward one night and return under the cover of darkness the next.

Sometimes a mission is even riskier. That same Sgt. John Mulcahy who photographed the bursting shell recently was convoyed by a special patrol to a prospective observation post (OP) in No Man's Land. Throughout the daylight hours he remained there alone. That night, under cover of darkness, a second patrol retrieved him. Another terrain specialist is Sgt. Robert Tacey of Binghamton, N.Y., who has skimmed low over enemy positions in light observation planes more than 24 times.

The civilian background of APS photographers ranges from years of service with metropolitan newspapers and newsreels to a dilettante amateur interest. Almost all plan to continue photography after the war. Photo agencies newsreels and movie studios keep a close watch on the men and photographic unions have promised to ease membership requirements.

The Army ranks on about the same par with photographers as it does with any GI but they admit only two persistent complaints.

One is the question asked each a dozen times daily: Are you with The Stars and Stripes? They've finally given up on that one and just answer. "Yes."

The second concerns pictures snapped under dangerous conditions which look as though they were taken from the rear.

For example, Sgt. **Burke O'Connell** of Nashville, Tenn., once was pinned down by machine guns after accompanying a patrol five miles, ahead of our advancing infantry. His companions decided that one man would break and run for it every five minutes. To quiet his jittery nerves, O'Connell photographed each frantic dash for safety.

A few days later a colonel called O'Connell in and blustered: "Why waste film on something that's no good? All your pictures show is a guy running—nobody can see the machine gun bullets."

LGR /mw

HEADQUARTERS FIFTH ARMY
Office of the Signal Officer
Army Pictorial Service
APO 464 U.S. ARMY

29 March 1945

APS BULLETIN
No. 2
TO: All photographic personnel

1. We are faced with a critical shortage of photographic supplies; motion picture film, film packs and cut film, flash bulbs, paper, chemicals, replacement parts for cameras, etc. In this connection, the attached Fifth Army circular is self-explanatory. It was executed in an effort to conserve our present stocks of photo supplies, and to reduce the demands made upon us for coverage unessential to the war effort.

2. It will be necessary for us to carry out further economies in our own coverage—mainly by the exercise of restraint, editorial judgment and common sense. Our work is evaluated here and by the War Department in terms of *quality* as well as quantity; not by the amount of footage or number of pictures as much as how well the coverage tells the story. These facts should be kept in mind when you approach a subject for coverage. Is it interesting? Has it "spot news" value? Does it convey anything of possible interest to the War Department? Will it contribute anything to the war effort? Does it have a tactical or technical value?

3. Combat material still remains the topmost category of what is demanded of all photographers in the field. But better planning should go into this coverage if it is to be of value to the War Department and the newsreels and papers. The advance of infantry is always interesting, but the supporting arms should be considered and covered whenever possible in order to present a complete picture of operations. The geography of operations is likewise vital for the historical record and other purposes; we must continue to identify on film each town that is taken.

4. Human interest material, and "home town news" coverage is still required of us, and is important. But each picture should be interesting in itself and, if at all possible, should serve more than one purpose; that is, should illustrate some military function as well as portray an individual or a group.

Pvt. Jones operating a machine gun or a bulldozer is far better than Pvt. Jones just staring into space.

Good human interest material is always at a premium, eagerly considered by papers and newsreels, more than often in preference to just ordinary forward area material.

5. The coverage of entertainments, USO shows, sporting or social events, sentimental group pictures, and purely routine activities of troops will be avoided. Requests for such coverage will be referred to APS or Corps representatives. This likewise applies to coverage of civilians except under combat conditions. Dramatic coverage of refugees, the suffering and devastation caused by war, should be evaluated from the standpoint stressed in paragraph 2.

6. Motion picture coverage of ordinary decorations and awards ceremonies will be restricted to "key shots"—but should be evaluated from the point of view of the importance of the award that is given. Naturally, full coverage will be given a soldier receiving the Medal of Honor. Common sense and circumstances should govern your coverage of such material. *Close still coverage* will be given these ceremonies, mainly for "home town news" purposes.

7. Coverage of bridge building, road building or repair, Quartermaster activities, Ordnance functions, will be considered from the standpoint of whether such material, in each case, presents anything new, unusual, or of value to the War Department from a technical or tactical point of view. Purely routine coverage of such activities should be avoided unless such coverage is illustrating combat conditions.

/s/ LINDEN G. RIGBY
Major, Signal Corps
Photo Officer

HEADQUARTERS
FIFTH ARMY SIGNAL SERVICE
ARMY PICTORIAL SERVICE
APO #464 U.S. ARMY

LGR / shl
16 April 1944

PHOTO MEMO NO. 4: "Home Town Coverage."

TO: : All Still Photographic Personnel

1. In spite of recent memos concerning still picture captions there continues to be a flow of incomplete and carelessly prepared captions from cameramen. All cameramen will take immediate steps to remedy this situation. The important rules to be followed are repeated below:

    a. All names, in full, will be printed in CAPITAL letters, including the "home town." Rank of individuals will be included.
    b. A brief but *accurate* personal background concerning subject will be included citing home address, civilian occupation, length of service in the Army, service overseas, military job and items of human interest that always exist. Getting the latter is largely dependent upon the ingenuity of the cameraman in "getting to" the subject or his buddies.
    c. Every effort will be made to attach a copy of the citation with the caption in cases of decorations.

2. Technically, the coverage of the "home town" type has, in general, been acceptable and above average. However, in order to further improve these pictures, more attention should be given to:

    a. *Exposure.* Check carefully in order to make it accurate.
    b. *Subject animation*—A man doing something is far more interesting than a man who is obviously "mugging" the camera. This problem necessitates clever selection of angles in order to keep the face of the subject prominent and recognizable.
    c. *Revealing identity of organizations and equipment*—Exercise care in selecting camera angles and backgrounds in order to eliminate identifying marks such as signs, shoulder patches, etc. Censorship prohibits, in many cases, releasing such material for "home town" distribution. Organizations should be included in the caption material only. (Note: Some items of

equipment that are commonplace within the theater, but not releasable for reproduction in news channels include the multi-barreled .50 caliber machine gun, 8-inch howitzer, 57mm gun, half tracks with combination 37 mm and .50 caliber machine guns, rocket guns (not including (bazooka), Bailey bridges, radar equipment, and close-ups of gun mechanisms.)

  d. *Crop in the camera*—Move in, filling the negative with subject material thus insuring recognizable faces upon reproduction.
  e. *Placement of subject*—Keep faces out of heavily shaded areas.
  f. *Grouping*—Whenever possible, attempt to get two or three people in the picture from the same "home town" area. i.e., area covered by the same newspaper. *All* names, etc., must be included in captions of group pictures of this type.

3. This is written with full realization of the hardships encountered by cameramen in the field. It should be born in mind, however, that for "home town" distribution, the best pictures are worthless unless accompanied by *complete and carefully prepared captions.*

/s/ LINDEN C. RIGBY
Major, Signal Corps

RESTRICTED

HEADQUARTERS
196Th SIGNAL PHOTOGRAPHIC COMPANY
APO 464, US ARMY

2 May 1945

ORDERS:　　　　　)
　　　　　　　　　:
NUMBER　　　　48)

1. The following named Off and EM will proceed a/a 5 May 45 from present sta on Temporary Photographic Mission to 10th Mountain Division. Orgn to which Off and EM are atchd for rations will be reported to this Hq; any subsequent changes will likewise be reported. Two (2) 2-1/2 ton 4x4 trucks, two (2) ¼-ton trailers, photographic equipment, and personal baggage will accompany Off and EM. Upon completion of mission or reld by Photo Off, Fifth Army, Off and EM will return to proper sta. GMT auth.

2d Lt.	FRANCIS P. MULHAIR
Tec. 3	Donald Wiedenmayer
Tec. 4	Marshall H. Bull
Tec. 4	Edmund B. O'Connell
Pfc.	Joe Cardinallo
Pvt.	James S. Morris

/s/ NED R. MOREHOUSE
Captain, Signal Corps
Commanding

(Army Service Number omitted)

HEADQUARTERS
196Th SIGNAL PHOTOGRAPHIC COMPANY
APO 464, US ARMY

30 May 1945

ORDERS:)
NUMBER 65)

EXTRACT

1. The following named Officers and Enlisted Men will proceed from present station on/about 30 May 45 as advance party to 180th Signal Repair Detachment for the purpose of processing equipment. Two (2) 2-1/2 ton 6x6 trucks, one (1) ¼-ton 4x4 truck, and (1) ¼-ton trailer, photographic equipment and personal baggage will accompany Officers and Enlisted Men. Upon completion of mission Officers and Enlisted Men will return to proper station. GMT auth:

1st Lt.	EDWARD R. AGER
S. Sgt.	Ralph E. Thomas
Tec. 3	Donald Wiedenmayer
Sgt.	Samuel T. Tischler
Tec. 4	Alfred Feuer
Tec. 4	Paul D. Graning
Tec. 4	Edmund B. O'Connell
Pfc.	Adolph J. Pollock
Pfc.	Herbert A. Schultz

/s/ Ned R. Morehouse
/t/ NED R. MOREHOUSE
Captain, Signal Corps
Commanding

A TRUE EXTRACT COPY
/s/ Philip F. Falcone
1st Lt., Signal Corps.

(Army Service Number omitted)

Bibliography

Butcher, Harry C., **My Life With Eisenhower**, New York, New York, Simon and Schuster, 1945.

Fisher, Ernest F. Jr., **Cassino to the Alps: U.S. Army in World War II: Mediterranean Theater of Operations**, Washington, DC: Center of Military History, 1989

Garland, Albert N.; and Howard McGraw Smyth, **U.S. Army in World War II: The Mediterranean Theater of Operations: Sicily and the Surrender of Italy**, Washington, DC: Center for Military History, 1993.

Hatlem, John C. and Hunter, Kenneth E., ed. **The U.S. Army in World War II (Volume II): The War Against Germany and Italy: The Mediterranean and Adjacent Areas,** Washington DC: Center For Military History, 1951. Second edition, 2005

Maslowski, Peter, **Armed With Cameras: The American Military Photographers of World War II,** New York. Free Press, 1993.

Meyers, Capt. Bruce A., **Fifth Army History, Part VI, Pursuit to the Arno,** 5 June-15 August 1944, Milan, Italy, Pizzi and Pizio, 1945

Morris, Eric, **Circles of Hell: The War in Italy 1943-1945,** New York, **Crown Publishers, Inc., 1993**

Raines, Rebecca Robbins, **Getting the Message Through: A Branch History of the U.S. Army Signal Corps,** Washington, DC: Center for Military History, 1996

Schmidt, Robert H., **The Forgotten Front in Northern Italy: A World War II Combat Photographer's Illustrated Memoir of the Gothic Line Campaign,** Jefferson, North Carolina, McFarland & Company, Inc., 1994.

Starr, Chester G., ed., **From Salerno to the Alps,** Nashville, Tennessee: The Battery Press, Inc., 1986

Thompson, George R., **The Signal Corps: The Test** (December 1941 to July 1943), Washington DC: Center for Military History, 2003.

U.S. Army, **19 Days: From the Apennines to the Alps: The Story of the Po Valley Campaign,** Milan, Italy: Pizzi and Pizio, 1945

U.S. Army, **Finito! The Po Valley Campaign 1945,** Milan, Italy: Rizzoli E.C., 1945

Zanuck, Darryl K., **Tunis Expedition,** New York, Random House, 1943